CHURT: A MEDIEVAL LANDSCAPE

CHURT
A Medieval Landscape

P. D. Brooks

Churt: a Medieval Landscape

First published 2000 by P. M. Heather
This revised edition published 2006

Typeset and published by John Owen Smith
19 Kay Crescent, Headley Down, Hampshire GU35 8AH

Tel: 01428 712892 – Fax: 08700 516554
wordsmith@johnowensmith.co.uk
www.johnowensmith.co.uk

ISBN 1-873855-52-4

Printed and bound by Antony Rowe Ltd, Eastbourne

Contents

Illustrations

১৯৯১৯

Philip Brooks, 1910–2000

About the Author

Philip Brooks was born in Leicester in 1910 and first developed an interest in agriculture when his father, a well-known scientist, bought Holywell Farm, not far from the city. As a result, Philip went to agricultural college, but could not find permanent work because, at the time, farming was severely affected by the Great Depression of the 1930s.

Consequently, he first worked in South Africa and later in Argentina where he was involved in clearing forest and managing orange plantations. He returned to Britain towards the middle of the Second World War and joined the RAF, remaining in the forces until virtually the end of the war.

After a brief return to Argentina, he came back to Britain and after working in several other places, came to Churt in 1950, taking a job as farm manager for Col. Rose at Old Kiln Farm. His interest in documentary history started as a result of examining deeds while purchasing parcels of land in Churt to expand Col. Rose's landholding. This led him to become involved on several archaeological excavations and on his retirement in 1974, having moved next door to the bungalow, he devoted himself to the study of the history of Churt. In this, as in nearly everything else, he was helped greatly by his wife Mary, whom he had originally met at college and who sadly died in 1999.

Initially, this interest led him to help with the work of the Domestic Buildings Research Group (Surrey) in recording the remarkable numbers of surviving Tudor buildings in the surrounding area. However, increasingly his attention was drawn to the documents preserved in the Hampshire Record Office in Winchester and in particular to the Winchester Pipe Rolls – the great medieval account rolls of the bishops of Winchester.

Philip mastered the intricacies of medieval Latin and over a number of years produced a series of articles on life in the medieval Hundred of Farnham. He became well known to a wide audience for the scope of his research and he opened the eyes of many people to the rich source of information to be found in the medieval and Tudor records. He is particularly authoritative on agricultural matters, as almost uniquely he has first-hand experience of clearing forest and of the use of traditional farming techniques. This knowledge has given Philip a remarkable insight into the world described by the medieval bishopric accounts – a world of ox plough teams, hand sown crops and a community whose very survival was entirely dependent on the produce of the land.

Philip Brooks died in June 2000.

David Graham

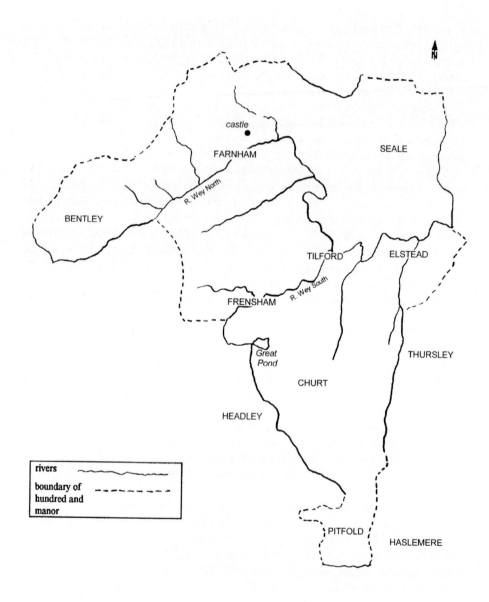

1: The Manor of Farnham showing the location of Churt

Preface

An alternative title for this book could be 'The Surrey Peasant' from which most people who have an interest in local history will realise my titles owe a compliment to the works of W G Hoskins. Hoskins, above all others, saw the countryside not merely as a full-scale map: he found banks and hedges interesting because he thought of the people who made them as much as why they were made. It was this sense of seeing the land from the inside which he was able to convey in his writing that brought it nearer to the reader. It did the same for me when I read 'The Midland Peasant'. Before that, collecting flints, living alongside a Roman camp and a holy well had been fascinating, but were disconnected fragments of history. Indirectly Hoskins showed me the way forward as did Robo in his book 'Medieval Farnham'. The 'Midland Peasant' is based on the village of Wigston, some four miles south of Leicester. It was in those Wigston fields that I spent the first 15 years of my life; fields then rich with cowslips on the damp land by the willows, willows as old as the Domesday book; fields below the footpath to Knighton Church where we children hunted quaking grass on the way home and ate the seedheads, whilst towards the Washbrook, corncrakes croaked on summer days. That was our England. This echo of W G Hoskins' work is intended as a tribute to one who would have done so much better with this story of Churt.

So many people have had a part in making this story of medieval Churt that it would be invidious to name one and miss another. Therefore, I thank all those people of Churt who have shared their memories with me and who have allowed me to roam their fields and invade their homes.

I owe an immense debt to the staff, now largely dispersed, of the old Hampshire Record Office (HRO) for so many happy hours reading the Pipe Rolls. In particular Miss Cash whose encouragement meant so much on first visits there; and also Mr Roger Davy for his patience with my first floundering efforts with medieval Latin.

Audrey Graham's contribution has been vital. After two other attempts had failed, she produced for me 'The Bishop's Tenants', a record of medieval peasant inheritance and land holding in the manor of Farnham. It is the core from which this story has evolved. Part of the preliminary text for this story was put on computer by Carolyn Clarke, an old friend from Pipe Roll days;

thereafter the work was continued by Pat Heather as it was easier for us to meet for regular discussions. The presentation and maps are her work and she has also made a valuable contribution in using her own work on Farnham to probe my ideas and to suggest alternative constructions. It would be true to say that without me this story would never have been started, and without Pat it would never have been finished.

Lastly, on a personal note, I must record my debt to the late Col. Rose of Old Kiln and the Rose family, but for them I should never have come to Churt; and lastly, above all, my debt to Mary, my wife.

Philip Brooks
Oakhurst, Churt
November 1996

Note: Field numbers quoted in the text (eg OS 898) refer to those on the Ordnance Survey First Series (1870) maps.

Churt

It may seem impossible that a village which did not exist a hundred years ago should have a medieval history and, of course, it is impossible. Nevertheless the land on which it stands and what is generally regarded as its parish does have such a history; not only that but it also has documentary links with a Saxon past. Churt, a village six miles south of Farnham in Surrey, is just such an oddity. Indeed it might well be described as 'the village that never was'! Even the name describes not a place but a whole district from Frensham to Shottermill: at least that is how the Saxons regarded it. The definition of 'Cert' is usually rendered as 'stony or scrubby'; however, the late Professor Dodgson of University College, London, wrote in a personal letter that for this particular corner of West Surrey, 'poor' was a better translation. In Churt the areas of poor common land are more extensive than the few stony places. Only by the chance location of school and church did what is now known as Churt village come into existence; a case of the right place at the right time. Every feature of every countryside has its own local history. Churt's peculiar distinction arises from the rare circumstance that so much of its medieval history has survived in written records; not only have they survived, being part of the incomparable Winchester Pipe Rolls, but the geographical and geological nature of Churt has aided reconstruction of the medieval landscape.

This work has its origin in a wish to know about the land I had been farming, and its catalyst was the recording of the old Churt houses by the Domestic Buildings Research Group (DBRG) some twenty years ago. To these reports I added notes culled from documents kept at the HRO, and at the time it seemed possible to extend these into a booklet on post-Tudor Churt. After several false starts it became obvious that the documentation was far too copious for such a booklet. It was even more so when I began reading the local accounts in the Winchester Pipe Rolls. The turning point came when I realised that the fines of land that I was translating began to tell the story of the fields I was farming. My interest then transferred from the houses alone to their builders and the land that had given rise to them. With my knowledge of pre-tractor farming it also became possible to appreciate how the Churt landscape of seven and eight hundred years ago had come into being from the needs of man and animal. Understanding of the location and size of nearly every medieval farm in Churt, combined with the records of crops and animals on the demesne farm of the castle in Farnham, provide a good idea of the pre-Black Death economy of a small, compact rural community. Comments on medieval farming and the landscape formerly scattered through this work, collated and expanded, became the main part being perhaps of wider interest than the purely local ramble around the village. In the event the importance and significance of Churt when considered as a whole outweighed the interest in any of its individual parts.

This is not the end of the story of Churt, merely a beginning. There is so much more to be discovered and understood; new information continues to come forward, confirming previous ideas or prompting new concepts. Without the Pipe Rolls this would be like many other local histories – dead; but with them it is possible to 'see' the old Churt – at least in imagination. It is a poor soul who, standing today on John of Hale's bank by Frensham Pond or contemplating the tangle that Andrew of Outmoor saw as a young hedge, cannot ponder on their lives.

The Pipe Rolls, for the historian a record of the bishop's riches, are for a curious countryman a story of the common people of England, with their ploughing, harvests, quarrels, misdemeanours and family relationships – 'the short and simple annals of the poor'. Of course, in one way, what we have is just a tiny flicker of light across the centuries but it may have some value beyond Churt, making it impossible to look at other landscapes of England without realising they too had such stories – if only we could find them.

The Landscape

Before the middle of the 20th century, local histories were usually written by a parson or some resident professional man; most, by later standards, amateurish. Since that time, increasing interest in all subjects embraced by local history has led to specialisation. Whilst this has yielded valuable results, it has also, on occasion, encouraged a narrow view of the subject as a whole. As an example, the recording of houses and their ancillary buildings has had, and is having, a dramatic effect on their preservation. Nevertheless, it is sometimes forgotten that the origin of the house and its existence depended ultimately on the land – first the land, second the dwelling. Local history used to be looked down on as something divorced from real history; it sometimes still is today, a view of crashing ignorance and error since all history of everyone and everywhere depended on the slave, peasant or bond-man producing a surplus of basic food above his own needs. Naseby, although a battle of considerable historical consequence, was to villagers on the hill very much a local event. Even Napoleon, who enunciated the principle on which his armies marched, demonstrated before Moscow the consequences of ignoring it.

One might wonder, therefore, why such an obvious and basic part of the subject as farming has been so regularly absent from comprehensive local studies. Books and papers without number have been written about farming in all its aspects. Complementing them are numerous works which describe the evolution of the landscape. To a large extent, the separation of aspects of the general subject has been inevitable. When the first local histories were written, farming was hardly considered of much interest, except perhaps when commenting on old or quaint customs. Now, those who write rarely have enough practical knowledge to avoid agricultural non sequiturs. The existence of the customary acre was unknown to most writers in the early part of the century. If any of them had possessed practical knowledge, the seed rate would have alerted them immediately; and some of Walter of Henley's[1] wilder assertions (these appear to have been inserted by a later hand) on ploughing would not have passed unnoticed.

Some of this criticism may be harsh. The difficulties of writing on early medieval farming are considerable; most of the documentary information

15

comes from sources which do more to record the results of farming rather than farming itself. The reader therefore has to decide what the writer meant. This in turn requires some knowledge of the old horse- or ox-farming as well as of the text. When early farming is discussed, only too often generalisations are quoted as if they applied equally everywhere. In some books dozens of examples are quoted from diverse sources, all without adequate context and with alarming conclusions. The essence of English farming is, and was even more so, its diversity not only by region or parish but also within the lands of individual farms.

There is a more important aspect to this. Most studies of landscape view it from outside. They demonstrate how to look for, recognise and understand clues from hedge and bank. This study does the reverse. With knowledge of the last years of the old horse farming and experience of farming in Churt, it has been possible to see the landscape from inside. What follows is therefore an attempt to unravel a little of the story of medieval Churt, and to show how farming created its landscape and is now destroying it.

Maps, Documents and Fieldwork

The three essentials for study of the landscape are good maps, complementary documents and stout boots; the first can be satisfied everywhere by the acquisition of the (first) 25 inch OS map 1870 and succeeding revisions. For many places a tithe map of circa 1830–1840 has survived. Though not as accurate, it may provide, as in Churt, the first evidence of the wholesale removal of hedges. Earlier maps, estate or otherwise, are often valuable in providing minor clues. Bryant's map of Surrey, for instance, proved that there was a 'Brown's' in Churt as well as in Frensham.

Twelve sheets of the 1870 edition of the OS map are needed to cover the whole of Churt. If these can be spread out together and viewed from above, they show the outlines of a Churt which is now largely destroyed or obscured by vegetation. Churt can be seen to be a sharply delineated island in a sea of commons. The Green Lane on the south, with Thursley Road and Jumps Road on the north, mark its extent in those directions, as well as the limits of the Bargate Bed of the Lower Greensand. In between are the north-south roads which whilst connecting the Upper and Lower Commons also preserve old farm boundaries. Around the edges of this 'island', are small invasions into the waste or common recorded as assarts before 1348. Within this general pattern, the maps show hedges and hedge lines of a curious regularity. Perhaps what is most surprising to see, and find, is that there are or were considerable differences between east and west Churt. In an earlier version of this text, an attempt was made to treat Maps, Fieldwork and Documents as separate subjects, but this proved impossible as each depends too much on the others. A great deal can be accomplished with a map and fieldwork alone. Banks and erosions do not always feature on maps whereas, and more importantly, the significance of longer or intact boundaries can only be arrived at from old maps as many are now incomplete on the ground.

16

Although maps are essential, even the best are limited in the information they can provide without documentary support. In Churt the interpretation of the countryside from field and map alone would have produced an entirely false picture. The difference between the field boundaries of east and west Churt would be obvious. But the long wandering ones at Hide (*see Fig 16*) would have been difficult to understand, nor could the enclosures of Hale and Hidland be understood without some knowledge of local medieval assarts. Even more vividly, the long hedge lines at Barford] could never have been seen as relics of numerous tiny fields. Only because documents like the Pipe Rolls exist does a faint idea of early Churt emerge: Gunora's trouble over her ox only becomes real when one realises that the ways they trod are the roads that our cars speed over today. Most localities have some documentation which, if lucky, goes back to the Tudor period. Beyond that there is rarely much more than the names of old sites and disconnected fragments. It was therefore of particular interest to see how far conclusions drawn from field and map study of Churt would stand up when compared with the riches of the Pipe Rolls. On the whole, they do not compare well. This is borne out by a reappraisal of my notes made without the benefit of information from the Pipe Rolls, which formed part of the reports on a number of houses in Churt by the Surrey Domestic Buildings Research Group. The notes were seldom completely wrong but did not contain 'the whole truth'.

Extract from a Pipe Roll of 1252–1253. Translation of the underlined words: "And of 13½d from Robert of Bereford for 4½ acres at Chert And 4½ d from Richard of …" ('Bereford' was Barford)

Some of the most important parts of the Pipe Rolls are those which deal directly (or indirectly, like heriots) with farm animals and crops. Professor Titow extracted the information for arable crops: the now classic 'Winchester Yields'[2]. It was my dream to do the same for animals, but like most dreams it never came true. Nevertheless a considerable amount of this matter has been extracted from the accounts of the manors of Farnham, Bentley, Frensham Beale and the demesne at Seale[3]. The heriots for the tithing of Churt from 1217 to circa 1400 have also been extracted. Details in the Rolls of the cows and sheep have also been observed for considerable periods to obtain an idea of fertility and survival rates. With this information and that from local inventories 1550–1600, some idea of early medieval farming emerges – not only what was theoretically possible but what the virgators probably achieved – something rather different from what we were formerly taught.

Amongst the results arising from this study of the documents and maps together with fieldwork were the recognition of the Saxon and Norman plough lands of High Churt and the identification of bondland and purpresture. From this stemmed some tentative dating of clearance of the waste, a boundary sequence and the location of the medieval farm sites and their correlation with the present landscape. More narrowly, it put in place the 'how and why' of William the Wayte's land and suggested a solution to the problem of the Hale House land. Without these documents, the significance of the long boundaries which enclose fields OS 898, OS 896 and OS 860 *(see Fig 4)* between Hale House Lane and Jumps Road would not have been explained as a late enclosure of a piece of old woodland or common.

What follows is an attempt to describe those features of the landscape of Churt which still survive and were created by and for the purpose of farming. In those days hedges were not regarded as enhancing the beauty of the countryside or channels for disseminating wildflowers or wildlife, both of which caused trouble. They were strictly utility appendages to be made, altered or obliterated as needs arose. History shows that this is exactly what happened. Open fields were enclosed and made smaller, and small ones enlarged, not randomly but responding over some eight centuries to the price fluctuations of corn, cattle and sheep, and changes of population.

Woods and Water

If one were to describe the medieval landscape of Churt as one of small farms set among great oak woods watered by fast flowing streams in every valley, it is likely that the description would be regarded as more lyrical than historical. Nevertheless that is what is implied by the Farnham Accounts in the Pipe Rolls. The existence of the oak woods is fact as there are numerous details of timber, not only for use at the castle and the mills in Farnham but also of timber taken to Esher[4], Southwark,[5] and other places. The fast-flowing streams owe nothing to imagination. Many of their courses can still be traced, whilst repeated damage to the dams of the ponds at Frensham and to the manorial mills leaves little doubt as to the force and quantity of the water involved.

The exact location of the oak woods was never recorded. From observation today it is clear that oak grows freely[6] over all parts of Churt. As the central part of Churt was occupied by identifiable medieval farms, the oak woods must have been on the Upper and Lower Commons *(see Fig 6)*; of these, for reasons given below, the Upper Common appears to be most likely. This is supported in a minor way by a few fines for land which contain the expression 'atte wode'[7]. In every case the land was at or above the Green Lane near Greencroft or Butts Farm.

The best medieval farms stretched northwards between the Green Lane and the Hale House – Thursley lanes. In every case except Outmoor, the site of the house was at the upper end of the land along the Green Lane. This would not have been possible unless adequate water had been readily available from a stream or a well; of the latter there is no information but streams were in the valleys, near at hand, in every case.

During the 13th, 14th and 15th centuries the destruction of the oak woods continued with little interruption as far as is known. The inevitable result was a drastic lowering of the water table with streams gradually receding down the valleys, probably with a long 'winter bourne' stage. The houses of the 'new build' after 1500 therefore required a new provision for water which resulted with the sinking of wells of 100ft or more in depth, some have been discovered recently. It may be due to chance or geological strata that the bottom of these wells along the Green Lane is almost exactly level with the water sources that now emerge, or used to emerge along the line of Hale House Lane.

In the last forty years many wet places, streamlets and springs have dried out completely. Until about 1960 water flowed freely down Greencross Lane and Old Barn Lane in all but the driest summers; now channelled underground there is nothing more than infrequent run-off after storms. One can hardly picture the dam of Frensham Pond being carried away by the present trickle of water down the Barford stream, yet it happened repeatedly in former times. One spectacular piece of evidence, now obliterated, was a washed-out valley under The Meadows estate[8]: the Bargate stone projecting from the sides of the minor 'ravine' showed how it had been formed.

Streams, Ponds and Wells

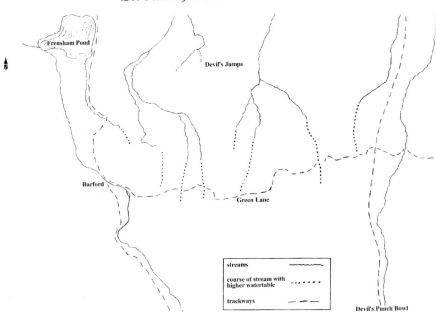

2: Streams in the Churt area

The map on the previous page shows the former main water courses, all of which originated from a series of springs along the north side of the Hindhead ridge. On the west, several flow into the Great Pond, most of the others collect and enter the Small Pond. There were also a few minor springs whose outlets move from time to time[9]. One spring, 'le fonte' in Whitmore Vale, was mentioned several times in the 13th century; the water flow must have been considerable to merit treatment as a landmark.

The locations of wells and ponds[10] are marked on several editions of OS maps but none has a complete record of their existence. Some wells are not recorded, such as those at Hide and Greencroft, no doubt because they are under the kitchen part of the house; others perhaps, like those in the lower parts of Churt, because they were shallow and could be filled in and re-dug without difficulty. The few wells that are in isolated positions are particularly interesting as they usually mark the site of a former house, although they may be replacement wells for those that have run dry or become foul. One such isolated well is marked as being on the green opposite Redhearn, one at Beefolds opposite the Old Post Office and another at Hitchin Croft adjacent to Butts.

The wells along the Green Lane require a special mention. The three that have been uncovered in the last twenty years, at Hide, Warryners and Greencross, are all over 100ft deep; the first two are very neatly lined with small stones whilst the third is lined with Tudor bricks. The sinking of these wells required considerable expertise and was not something that could be lightly undertaken, because of the nature of the work and the cost. Although it is difficult to find evidence to date these wells, it is probable that they date from the sixteenth century 'new building' period. Hide, for instance, was vacant before 1503. The well under the kitchen end of the house may be contemporary with the new house built by the Luffes at that date, or as a 'home improvement' when the new wing was added a hundred years later.

Ponds, like wells, are also only marked on a few map editions[11]. This is not surprising since apart from the few deeper ones they were easily dug and could quickly silt up when disused. Ponds were often within farmyards, for example at Greencross and Hide. The pond in the farmyard makes a pretty picture of former rural life if one is unaware that it was all too often a filthy source of disease to both man and animal. Before piped water was brought in, ponds were of great importance. Most were open to all cattle. When the commons were enclosed, a special clause stated that the pond opposite Old Kiln should be left open for all livestock. The wayside pond is seldom now recognised as such. Until recently all animal movement was on foot; livestock of any kind even going to the local market might have to travel ten to twelve miles. It was essential to have regular watering places so that animals did not become dehydrated and then drink too much whilst heated. In Churt the many small streams which crossed its roads served this purpose. When bridges were built across the larger streams and small rivers the former fords were usually retained – cattle and teams could use them as watering places in passing[12]. The old steam traction engines also used the fords to replenish their water tanks.

Banks and Ditches

As written earlier, ditches preceded the banks and hedges. They could hardly do otherwise since the bank could not be raised without excavation of the soil from which it was built. Most have now been obliterated by the passage of time, though some have probably been deliberately filled. Examples can be found at the side of the road which runs from Frensham Pond to Simmonstone alongside the Barford Stream (*see below*). Twenty years ago when surveyed they were devoid of vegetation. These banks and ditches[13] are those made by the de Hale families in the 13th and early 14th centuries.

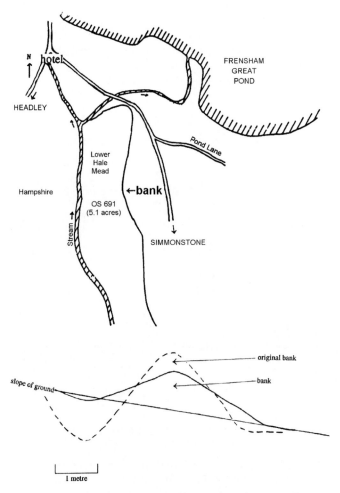

3: *John de Hale's bank near Frensham Great Pond*

Another bank along the footpath to Bookham's at The Furlong is still massive although the ditch has totally disappeared. There is some, though not conclusive, evidence that these ditches were carefully maintained up to the Black Death in the same fashion as the Midland ditches used to be, re-dug when the adjoining hedge was laid. The early 13th century Pipe Rolls contain many such references, for example digging out the old ditch (*fossa*) between Farnham and Bentley etc. One tends to forget that the old farmers were also tenants, and like modern ones could be held responsible and turned out for waste and destruction, as indeed they sometimes were.

Erosion Banks

Erosion banks arise from the natural movement of soil downhill. The rate of erosion is erratic, not only does it vary according to the steepness of a slope, but also to the nature of the soil and, not surprisingly, it can be greater on light land than on heavy land. There are also places where erosion is greater over short stretches of a long unbroken boundary, probably explained by the fact that the field below the bank was maintained as arable long after its neighbour was converted, or reverted, to grassland.

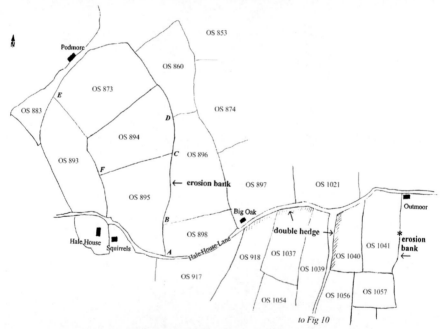

4: Erosion Banks and Double Hedges

An interesting example of erosion is the boundary which surrounds the valley between Hale and Old Kiln, shown on the map above[14]. Starting at the gate opposite Highfields (*A*) down to where the boundary meets an old bank (at *B*) was a typical Churt bank, some 3–4 ft high with a hedge on top. From

22

B to *C* the erosion bank steadily decreases in size, and from *C* to *D* it is even steeper. It then decreases until it disappears near Old Kiln. Opposite Podmore the bank becomes steep again. Field OS 893 is nearly level but the valley boundary between *E* and *F* used to be a vertical bank, from memory 6–8 ft high. Over the remainder of the boundary which finishes at Hale House Lane, the bank decreases as it meets the leveller land opposite Squirrels. The casual reader might ponder the fact that soil moving down at the rate of one eighth of an inch each year, something hardly measurable in the field, would easily account for the 8–10 ft banks formed around the enclosures made in Churt during the medieval period. One of the most spectacular examples can be found to the east of Greencross Lane in the south east side of OS 1041 *(marked with an * on Fig 4 and shown on the photograph below; see also Fig 8)* where erosion has lowered the level about 13ft. What used to be a field gently sloping to the north west is now nearly level.

5: An erosion bank on the west boundary of Outmoor.
*The post in the centre is 4ft high. (Position marked * in Fig 4.)*

Most of these banks are of some antiquity, though the extent of the erosion does not equate with age. Arable land on the lower side will increase the rate of erosion vastly more than permanent grass. Arable land on both sides of a hedge across a slope will further increase it. The examples quoted arose from normal farming activities.

The most obvious erosion banks are those along the roads. It is worth pausing a moment by Big Oak in Hale House Lane and visualising the road as it first was, rising as high as the tree's bole and descending eastwards to where the old stream flowed across in the valley.

Hedges

Before the middle of the 20th century, hedges had been of little concern outside farming circles. They were simply part of a stable landscape, made necessary by the needs of agriculture. To a slightly wider public, they were also a barometer of farming prosperity. Uncared-for hedges and the absence of a few stacks of old hay were certain signs of general or personal decay. After about 1950, hedges became the focus of mounting disquiet as their place in the history of the landscape came to be recognised. What had been more a lament by Hoskins and others developed into a battle where reason and history were discarded as irrelevant. Protagonists advanced their ideas with a virulence that often helped their antagonists' causes more than their own. On the farming side, there were still memories of the disasters after 1879, passed down through the generations, memories too of wasted fields after the repeal of the Corn Act in 1921 and of vacant farms and ruined friends of 1931. Against this background, interference from outside after a few years of prosperity came ill, hindering preservation of vital parts of the landscape. Opposed to farming were those who had come to realise that the landscape was just as valuable a record of history as the written document – and needed similar preservation. To make things more difficult, vociferous groups clamoured for a return to old ways and all manner of preposterous sectional interests. What neither side realised, at least at first, was that certain events had made the conflict inevitable, the first being the stark necessity after 1939 to produce food. The War Agricultural Executive Committees were instructed to brook no opposition[15].

The introduction of the tractor to farming did not just cause change as is often supposed – it marked a total break with the past. Never before had it been possible, at least theoretically, to introduce unlimited power and fertility to the countryside. The effects were all-pervading. Silage replaced hay. The horse disappeared and with it immense quantities of the manure which had formerly returned to the land. Rickyards were no more, and gone were the rats and mice that fed the owls and hawks, together with sparrows and all that had depended on them for winter food. This was balanced in turn by the replacement of the dreadful old farm cottages with modern ones and the introduction of electricity.

Hedge Laying

Modern hedge laying has developed in two ways, Southern and Midland. At first sight, the Southern looks to the Midlander to be a stupid method. In fact both methods respond to the needs of farming and farmers.

Midland hedges unless deliberately ruined were always composed of thorn, mostly planted in the 17th and 18th centuries when the old open fields were enclosed and new farms planned. Thorn was essential because of the change to mixed grassland and arable farming. Enclosure made it possible to take more livestock from upland areas for feeding and fattening. It was therefore necessary for the hedges to be stock-proof against mature cattle. The secret of the Midland method was to lay the hedge growth in such a way as to slope away from the worker. (There was nearly always a ditch on the working side which was re-dug when the hedge was finished and the spoil placed under the hedge. Finally the discarded hedge thorns were heaped into the ditch to protect new growth from cattle, later superseded by 'backfencing' with barbed wire.) When the hedge was finished, new growth started at every level, that from the bottom being unimpeded by the growth higher up. In the second and succeeding years, the new shoots were cut up the slope (one always cut up, never down). Each layer provided a mass of new growth and thorns, a real bullock-proof hedge.

6: Double hedge at Big Oak, Hale House Lane (see Fig 4):
Left–opposite Big Oak; right–the hedge at the back is a laid hedge

The Southern method, which also responded to the needs of the farmer was exactly the reverse of the Midland. Firstly it was (for the Churt hedges at least) very much earlier, many hedges being in place four or five centuries before the Midland enclosures. Secondly farming needs were different. The difference between the two methods was small, though the consequences were great. In the south, being woven round stakes the hedge was vertical instead of sloping. Laid in this way, hazel produces a massive growth of vertical wands, some subsequently incorporated in the hedge, the majority left to grow until suitable for coppicing. A second difference arose from the necessity to weave severed poles into the hazel hedge in order to make a better barrier. No dead material was ever incorporated into the Midland hedge, indeed great care was taken so that all the laid branches remained partly attached to the stumps or stovings as they were called.

Hedges in 1994

The best that can be said about the Churt hedges in 1994 is that they are the wreckage of a thousand years of farming – give or take a century or two. Prior to 1939, Churt had been essentially an area of small farms, some owned by the occupiers, others tenanted. Although some farming continued, the old ways had gone, in particular the care of the hedges which formerly had been a matter of some pride. For tenants it had also been a requirement written into the tenancy agreements. During the war, this lapsed and with a few exceptions no hedge had been laid in the old way for some sixty years. The present hedges therefore in no way resemble what Churt was like at the start of the 20th century, and even less the situation at the start of the 19th.

In order to get any idea of what hedges were really like, it is necessary to go back to the 1830s. Although not possible 'in the flesh', it can be done 'on paper'. This is because the tithe and OS maps show what occurred in the intervening years. In High Churt, hedges and banks were removed wholesale, two small fields being converted into one larger one; the removal of hedges is nothing new. Moreover the reason in the 1840s and 1950s was exactly the same, high corn prices. By the Hungry Forties, improvements in farming techniques, the four-course rotation, improved ploughs etc, and a growing industrial population, had made arable farming profitable, and in a place like Churt, being unsuitable for cattle with its poor land and small farms, far more profitable than animal farming. The result, as shown on the tithe map was

7: Ash poles from coppicing at junction of Greencross Lane and Hale House Lane

that nearly every ploughable field on the schedule was described as arable (even down to an odd triangle between the end of Hale House Lane and the Tilford–Hindhead road). Of more interest for this study is how the fields and hedges reflect the continuity and history of Churt.

Even the most cursory survey of hedges in Churt in 1994 reveals the fact that they consist almost entirely of hazel. In some places holly has invaded and there are small stretches where elm is re-colonising. Careful examination shows that the holly is a late invader. A few holly trees can be dated, mostly to the early 1930s. Holly now in the hedges shows the same growth. It all developed after regular hedge maintenance ceased and is destroying old hedges at an astonishing rate. Except to the practised eye, there is little evidence that the hedges were ever cared for or even mildly stock-proof. The clue that they were lies in the survival of a few ash stumps and, in a few places, the horizontal poles that were laid from them. One example can be found on the north side of Hale House Lane, a few yards from the entrance to Spring Gate Farm. I have coppiced these ash trees several times to provide poles some 2 inches thick and 8–10 ft long. When left to grow without spreading lateral branches, they provide splendid long timbers. Two ash trees at the bottom of Greencross Lane, on the Minfordd side, must be at least 50 years old (*see Fig 7*).

When this is allowed for, the fact remains that the Churt hedges consisted of a single species. According to the theory of hedge dating by species count, they should be relatively modern. In addition to containing only one species, the clumps of hazel show a regularity of spacing that cannot have come about by chance. It therefore poses the question, are these hazel hedges as old as the known ages of the fields they enclose?

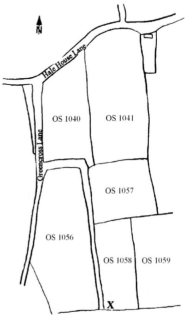

8: *Map showing location of photos at Figs 7 & 9 (see also Fig 10)*

The antiquity of the Churt hedges became an important question after hedges were found virtually intact in field OS 1105 (*see Fig 10*). The likelihood that these single-species hedges could have survived for 700–800 years was difficult to believe. Oliver Rackham[16] gives hazel as a regular component of old hedges but only as odd plants. I consulted Alan Mitchell[17] who was doubtful, bolstering my own thoughts. Richard Muir[18] was also cautious on the subject. Nevertheless documents have proved that the hedges are old, being maintained clean by regular coppicing, a practice unwittingly carried on by myself when farming in the 1950s, 1960s and 1970s – and in my garden hedge on Hale House Lane. *Since this was first written, fieldwork has shown that hazel has a smothering effect on briars etc. Ivy invades hedge banks when neglected but establishes itself slowly. Hedges coppiced on Old Kiln Farm in 1950–1955 are still virtually free of briars forty years later.*

Unless one believes that at some date the original hedges were replaced with hazel, one must accept that these hedges are as old as the fields they enclose. It has already been stated that the hedges and fields must complement the farming of the land. Hazel (which is always quoted as a constituent of old hedges) must therefore have been a useful adjunct to farming in Churt.

Spontaneous Hedges

This type of hedge is rarely mentioned separately, though it has a bearing on the subject of species counting. It derives from the space left along a boundary between neighbouring farms. As neither could in practice plough to the exact edge of his property without invading his neighbour's, a small strip remained unploughed. This in time, if neglected, became populated by a succession of tall grasses, briars etc, and finally seedling trees. In due course the volunteer growth became worth trimming into a hedge. Most are old, dating from when the plots first impinged on one another. On level land a good hedge is finally developed. When along a slope, the subsequent erosion bank often became a wide 'rew'. In several places, below the site of the Romano-British farm in Frensham Beale manor and on the east side of the Devil's Punchbowl, a succession of hedge lines mark old levels of adjacent fields. In Churt these spontaneous hedges rarely conform to species counting, being a random creation of wind, beast and man.

Double Hedges

These are thought to have been planted post-1500. The idea was to cut each side alternately. It maintained a good hedge in place while providing more harvestable material. Surtees, the famous writer on fox hunting, mentioned a similar practice in the Midlands in the early 19th century. Some of the hazel hedges in Churt were planted in double rows on top of substantial banks, of which only a few remain (there is a record of several removed in the 1950s.) Tentative dating of these hedges to the Tudor period now looks more probable from the cumulative evidence assembled whilst writing this study. Those that survive appear either to have divided land known to have been in use before the Black Death or filled gaps in 'open fields' ('open' in the context described in Gated Roads). The Hale land is a good example (*see Fig 4*) where the erosion banks which surround it show that it had long been cleared. The double hedge between OS 894 and OS 895 (now removed) was planted on a bank which impinged on erosion banks at either end in such a way as to prove that it was of a later date. All the internal banks have now disappeared.

A similar double hedge division still exists dividing an old assart above Green Lane between OS 1109 and OS 1135 (*see Fig 10*). Two others fill gaps between old erosion banks. One along the roadside opposite Big Oak, at the north west corner of OS 918 (*see Fig 4*), starts with a double hedge at the top (*See Fig 6*) and deteriorates through erosion by cattle to a single line to the east. The same in-fill took place with the double hedge between OS 1040 and OS 1056 that divided 'le gros felde' and joined up on the east with the erosion bank between OS 1041 and OS 1057 (*see Fig 8*).

9: The author standing beneath the end hazel of a hazel hedge at Greencross Lane, now the roadside hedge of 'Tilney'. The trees are all of about the same size and are unlikely to be less than 70 years in growth. The position of this hedge is shown at X in Fig 8.

Gated Roads

In some parts of the Midlands there used to be what were known as 'gated roads'. They originated from enclosure of the old open fields. As the ancient roads which served them could not usually be moved, a gate was needed to shut off each new field from the next. Farmers going to market often carried a boy on the back of their traps to open and shut the gates. At Shilton in Warwickshire, one field fenced on the roadside was called 'Open Close'.

Churt has, or had, several of these fields. Their distinguishing feature is the differing ages of the hedges on either side of the road. The best example is on Greencross Lane. The hedge and bank below The Toft (*see Fig 10*) is fairly modern – there is no trace of erosion on the field side of the bank. On the opposite side, the hazel hedge tops a considerable erosion bank. In former times there would have been a gate at each end of the lane. Old Barn Lane was probably much the same. The gate at the north end of it survived until about 1900.

Hedgerow Trees

The hedgerow tree rarely features in local history. It was too common to command attention – except perhaps when felled. Despite that, its presence enhances landscapes adding depth and scale, quite apart from the beauty of any individual tree in the fullness of its growth. One can hardly imagine

29

Constable's 'Cornfield' flanked by trees planted at the request of the local council! But who planted them? Why are they there?

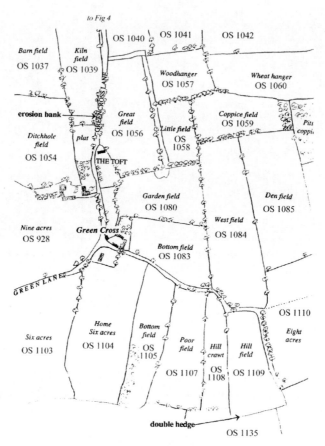

to Fig 4

OS 1040   OS 1041   OS 1042

Barn field   Kiln
OS 1037   field
              OS 1039   Woodhanger   Wheat hanger
                               OS 1057   OS 1060

erosion bank   Great   Coppice field   Pits
                   field   OS 1059   coppi.
Ditchhole   plat OS 1056   Little field
field   OS
OS 1054   1058
            THE TOFT

                             Garden field   Den field
                             OS 1080   OS 1085

Nine acres   Green Cross   West field
OS 928   OS 1084

                             Bottom field
                             OS 1083

GREEN LANE
                                                         OS 1110

             Home   Bottom   Eight
Six acres   Six acres field   Poor   acres
OS 1103   OS 1104   OS   field   Hill   Hill
                       1105   crawt   field

                       OS 1107 OS   OS 1109
                                1108

double hedge
                             OS 1135

10: Hedges at Green Cross

Although many banks and hedges have now disappeared, it is possible that the removal of trees growing along them has had the greatest impact on the landscape. References to single-species hedges are obviously wrong if one looks at the oaks and ashes in them today. Nevertheless there is evidence that they were single-species hedges, managed so that only desirable intruders were allowed to remain: oak, ash, and perhaps the odd elm being cropped in their turn as required. When I was taught hedge-laying many years ago in Warwickshire, it was customary to leave the odd good sapling. When finished it projected some feet above the hedge line, rapidly becoming a good young tree. No one was ever told to do it. No comment was ever made. The hedger neither gained nor lost. Not so the tenant (they were nearly all tenants in those days); to him trees could be a nuisance. They were

30

the landlord's property, not his. Corn in their shade failed and hay dried more slowly. He could easily have said, 'Take all the saplings out ...' but didn't. Although far away from Warwickshire, the Churt hedgerow trees probably grew from a similar tradition or practice. With more knowledge now, it seems probable that this was the continuance of the practice of leaving saplings to grow into standards where managed woods were coppiced, a practice, from evidence of the causeways of the Somerset Levels, that went back to the Bronze Age.

Woodland & Coppices

The practice of coppicing probably became important in the manor of Farnham when sources of wood and timber began to diminish. The distinction between wood and timber is important as it defines the customs and rights which governed relations between lord and bondman. These are, from lack of knowledge, usually referred to in general terms regardless of the fact that they must have differed in wooded and treeless areas. What is described below refers specifically to Farnham, being compiled from entries in the pre-1348 Pipe Rolls.

At the start of the 13th century the manor still contained considerable stands of timber, chiefly oak. Only on very rare occasions was ash or 'popelare' mentioned. Oteryngwode north of Farnham castle, and Kokenore on the west towards Alice Holt, were named woods. Churt was also a major source of oak. All timber was of great value and strictly reserved to the bishops of Winchester. The point was never elaborated in the accounts but it seems doubtful if bondmen had unrestricted use of fallen or broken wood in the woodlands as it was regularly accounted for and sold. Outside and on their own tenanted lands they did have certain rights. The principal one was for building material for their houses, a right tempered by the fact that the subsequent house belonged to the bishop. Nor could they take the required timber themselves; the trees were picked and marked by the woodwards. Neither did the bondmen burn wood on their fires. There was not enough to sustain such a practice over any long period. Turf was their usual fuel. Unlike woods which needed replanting to sustain them, local turf was self-generating to a large extent. The Yule log would not have become such a feature of Christmas if the burning of such logs had been the general practice.

During the 13th century, or at least during the first seven or eight decades, there was a steadily increasing population in the manor. This must inevitably have caused some diminution of woodland resources. At the same time, encroachments into Oteryngwode and specific felling of building oak were adding to the pressure on them. Not only was timber felled for work at the castle but large amounts were used for buildings at Esher and Southwark. In addition there was a constant need for lesser material for hurdles, sheepfolds, tools, panelling, minor building work and repairs. Oak being either too valuable or unsuitable was often replaced by hazel which grew well on the Farnham soils. One presumes that until the early 13th century, natural groves had supplied Farnham's needs; this may or may not be true. The fact remains that the early Rolls contain repeated references to enclosing coppices and fetching wood, presumed to be coppice wood, for minor works. It seems certain that natural groves were both being protected and added to. The main ones seem to have been in the (Old) Park. Other sources either natural or protected were in Churt and also near the Bourne mill.

Many years ago in the course of reading miscellaneous documents, I found references to tree felling on a more considerable scale than that referred to in the fine books. At the time they were not thought of much importance and few notes were taken. Some are now seen to have been part of the later great landscape clearance[19].

Concurrent with the expansion of population and probably the first serious inroads into the stocks of growing timber was the major devolution of land to tenants. According to the fines and new rents recorded in the Pipe Rolls of the first half of the 13th century, some of the later consolidated virgates of the tenants were made up bit by bit from small plots each of which, if from the waste (and probably from the demesne), needed demarcation. This was done as explained by ditch and bank. This was quite suitable as a formal bound-ary, but was of little use against animals. The bondman then had to make some kind of fence on his bank. Two methods were open to him, both long practised on the demesne. One method is exemplified by the great dead thorn barrier round the ditch of the castle and was sometimes used on other boundary banks. The other was the type of barrier used around the open cornfields; often there is no explicit description, nevertheless from comments on the repairs made they seem to have been a mixture of growing bushes and quasi-hurdles or dead wood. What the bondman did was to select from what he saw that best suited his purpose, hazel. Firstly it grew well on the West Surrey land. Secondly it made a sufficient barrier for the few animals he was able to keep, of which the house cow and horse were often tethered. Sheep caused no problems as they were in charge of a shepherd by day and folded by night, either in a wooden fold or in one of the small fields.

The hazel hedge suited the bondman in several ways. The most important benefit, and one which continued for many centuries, was to provide him with a source of coppice wood. It was not timber so he was able to use or sell it as he wished. It provided him with wood for tools, hurdles, any form of light construction, and fuel. And as he no doubt saw or came to see, coppicing his hedges, section by section, year by year, provided a source of use or gain unaffected by any of the normal vicissitudes of life. References to coppicing of hedges can be found in papers[20] concerning a dispute over tithes at Frensham in the last decade of the 18th century. The new Rector tried to revert to the old practice of collecting tithes in kind. This was opposed by the farmers. A case finally went to the High Court in London – the Rector lost. The most valuable parts of the papers are the depositions by witnesses, old inhabitants, as to what had formerly been done. Regarding hedges, it was deposed that there was some uncertainty but they believed that hedge material cut beyond a certain distance from the centre of the hedge was tithable, and it was the custom to make it up as follows:–

> long timber
> faggots and bavins in bundles of 25
> smooth rods and bough rods, 50s
> brush wood.

George Bourne (Sturt)[21] writing on local matters at the beginning of the 20th century tells of Bettesworth coppicing hedges during the winter.

The tithe map and schedule of 1839 shows numerous coppice fields adjacent to woods as well as specific identification of coppices. It would appear that virtually every available odd corner of land or whole wood was coppiced.

Regeneration of the Land

The following observations stray into the botanist's domain and invite correction. Nevertheless they do give an idea of what the sequence might have been following the dereliction caused by the Black Death in the 14th century. In the 20th century when farming in Churt began to decline after about 1950, odd pieces of land were left to weeds. The plant succession in the following thirty years provides an idea of what occurred on derelict land in earlier times. On ploughed land, ground weeds and birch were the first colonisers. On poor grass, gorse predominated with oak seedlings – as was taking place on Frensham Common at the same time. Something similar took place on the commons in the 17th and 18th centuries when year after year the bishopric estates documents record complaints about scrub and gorse invading commons, the old grazing management having virtually ceased. (A good idea of what hard-grazed commons were like is provided by the areas between the car park and the Ranger's house at Frensham Little Pond.)

A surprise, at least to me, was to find places where dense thickets of oak excluded virtually all other vegetation. In many years oak trees produce few acorns[22]. The field between Big Oak and Spring Gate Farm, OS 897 *(see Fig 4)*, was permanent grass from about 1960. In several years up to 1976 thousands of oak seedlings appeared in the spring. None attained more than 6 inches in height, being killed by grazing and mowing. One can only suppose that certain combinations of acorn crop, ground texture, and bird population caused such immense seeding over eight acres.

A few documents add point to these generalisations. A fine of 1451 relating to Stock Farm indicates that there at least land had returned to scrub. On the other side of the Hide Lane, fields called Heath Field and Broom Field may indicate something of their former condition. Another aspect arises from later references to woods on the lands of various people. There is no proof, but it suggests that only part of a farm was being used for farming, the rest having 'gone back' – or had never been cleared.

Removal of Hedges

The enlargement of the fields during the years between the tithe map survey and the first Ordnance Survey can be seen from the maps themselves. What occurred in the years before the tithe map was difficult to unravel. The first major find, many years ago, at the HRO was the Parliamentary Survey of Headley, 1552 which revealed that Headley consisted almost entirely of small fields[23]. Given the complementary nature of land and people it was difficult to imagine that the Churt fields were any different. Evidence for early assarts about Barford and elsewhere confirmed this view. Unless new land was cleared by more than one person or family as was done with the Furlong[24], the acreage was always small. This is exactly what practical experience would expect. It is easier to clear the land in the first place than bring it into cultivation and maintain it thus. The next find was the description of Woodyer's land in 1621 in the Wheeler Papers in which the fields there were just over 2 acres each. Even with this information it was difficult to believe from extant evidence that Churt really had been like its neighbour Headley. This only became clear with the belated discovery of the 1793 document[25] relating to Old Forge, then guesses became certainty: the whole landscape, banks, hedges and trees, which had been built up over a period of 800 years, had been swept away in a lifetime. Between 1793 and the tithe map of 1832 half the hedges had gone, doubling the size of the old fields to about 4 acres, and by 1870 they had again been doubled, leaving fields much as they are today[26]. Very roughly, the old two acre closes had given way to fields of about eight acres.

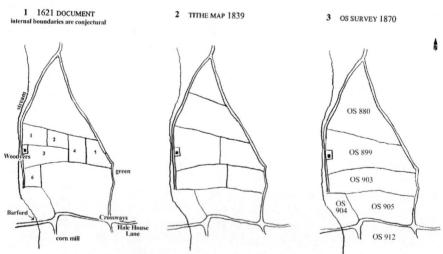

11: Changes to field boundaries at Woodyers

Two field names almost alone bear witness to Churt's former state; the field adjacent to The Toft and the field in the west opposite Greencroft, both of some 6 acres, bore the name in documents of 'le gros felde', the great field.

Beside this dramatic change, modern alterations pale into insignificance. It is therefore curious that no record of this change to the landscape has been preserved in local history. Even surprising that Cobbett did not make some comment. As a practical man he probably regarded a good harvest as more use to his fellow men than a nice view. Although presented here as Churt–Headley changes, they cannot have been unique. The forces that caused them were acting on farming everywhere. These changes have implications concerning the preservation or conservation of the present landscape. Selective decisions made without knowledge of previous history can easily result in the retention of a hedge actually planted in the 19th century – there are one or two.

Notes

[1] Walter of Henley: author of "Husbandry" a 13th century treatise on estate management.

[2] J Z Titow, Winchester Yields Cambridge University Press 1972

[3] Part of this has been published: P D Brooks, *Pigs, Pannage and Pestilence*, FMSN Vol. 10 page 4 (1983)

[4] 1314-15 Account: 14/- paid for 42 carts with 84 men taking timber from Churt to Farnham for building work at Esher. *HRO B1/70 159329* This entry is only one from amongst many. A good deal of timber was taken to Esher; none seems to have been available nearer.

[5] 1310-11 Account: 2 oak beams taken via Weybridge for the bishop's boat at Southewark, from the woods of John of Hide. *HRO B1/66 1594581/2*

[6] Frensham Common is a good example of how easily even poor land can be recolonised with oak without the usual interim stage of birch. There has been a significant growth of oaks on Frensham Common since the great fires of the 1950s.

[7] 1307: fine of 3/4d from Matilda daughter of William of the Wode for a messuage and half a virgate. (This is part of Butts Farm.) *HRO B1/63* 1308: fine of 5/- from John atte Wode for messuage and six acres of purpresture from Isabel atte Wode his mother. (This is "Greencroft".) *HRO B1/64*

[8] When this estate was being built in the 1960s, a sudden storm flooded the bottom bungalow up to the eaves.

[9] Two appeared suddenly in 1950 in the valley opposite Spring Gate Farm.

[10] See Map XIII pages 34-35 for list of ponds and wells in Churt.

[11] Some early OS maps are useful for showing ponds which have now disappeared.

[12] Bill Croucher, a farm worker in Churt, remembered the ford at "The Mariners" in Frensham being used in that way.

[13] The Hale banks by the Barford stream south of Frensham Pond need special mention. They are not only datable, something rare, but are possibly some of the best examples in West Surrey. They should be protected as an important heritage feature.

[14]Some of these banks were levelled c.1950 to make corn growing possible as then directed. They were riddled with rabbit burrows. Several oaks mark the old hedge lines.

[15]In at least one case a farmer who opposed change – and presumably lost his senses, was shot in his home.

[16]Oliver Rackham *Trees and Woodland in the British Landscape* 1976

[17]Alan Mitchell *A Field Guide to Trees of Britain & Northern Europe* 1974

[18]Richard Muir *Hedgerows: Their History & Wildlife* 1987

[19]The old Headley landscape was undergoing the same change as Churt. The Combe-Millers had land in both Churt and Headley. Among their papers at the HRO are two of which note was made; the first, a survey of timber in 1783 on Plaster Hill and Rooks Farms, along the Headley Lane; the second of 1794 gave details of individual trees felled, viz:– 116 loads of oak timber; 10 loads of ash timber; 5 loads of elm timber; 2 loads of beech timber

[20]Deposited at GMR

[21] "The Bettesworth Book" by George Sturt

[22]Throughout the 13th and 14th centuries the Pipe Rolls recorded the presence or absence of acorns for pannage.

[23]A rough calculation suggests an average of 3 acres or less per field.

[24]See Manorial Fines *page 51*

[25] Deposited in the Minet Library

[26]This is useful information which may apply to other areas e.g. how and why the small plots of land in Runwick granted in the 13th century, having survived exchanges in the 16th century, were finally amalgamated.

The Medieval Farming Year

The Demesne of Farnham Manor in 1223

Although there is an enormous literature on medieval farming in all its aspects, most of it betrays a lack of knowledge of actual farming[1] and its hazards. To redress this and to give the background to the way the Churt farms were cultivated, the various stages of cultivation are described below in some detail, and in particular the importance of hazards and difficulties. These hazards were the same for demesne and virgate; the scale of farming made no difference: the virgator of Churt would have suffered from slugs and weather just as much or as little as the bishop did on his demesne. The demesne of Farnham as recorded for the year Michaelmas 1223 to Michaelmas 1224 is compared with what it might have been like if farmed on the same scale in 1923[2].

Inventory

In 1223/4[3] the inventory of the livestock on the Farnham demesne as taken at Michaelmas was:

1223/4 Livestock

1 horse for the cart	78 oxen	19 young cattle	242 ewes
9 plough horses	29 cows	10 calves	251 wethers
	1 bull	– calved April 1224	138 ewe lambs

In 1923 the inventory would have been surprisingly similar though proportions of the various classes of animals changed. There would have been fewer sheep as flocks of wethers were no longer kept. Cattle numbers are likely to have been greater. Some of the oxen would have been fattened on the meadows. Dairy cow numbers might have been greater, with the progeny being raised on the poorer land.

The inventories of implements for the two periods:

1223/24 Implements	1923 Implements
1 cart	4 wagons
1 biga[4] – *may have been used mostly for the bishop's luggage*	2 digger ploughs
wooden ploughs with iron shares	3–4 iron single furrow ploughs
several harrows	heavy harrows
light or brush harrow	duck foot harrows
	medium harrows seed harrows
	1–2 seed drills
	roller

These are of course only the main implements that a 1923 farm would have had for arable cultivations. Steam engines with tackle for ploughing and cultivating were also readily available. Both the farm in 1223 and in 1923 would have had haymaking implements also: forks and scythes in 1223 and horsedrawn mowers, turners, tedders and rakes in 1923.

After spending hundreds of hours reading the Pipe Roll accounts of farming of the demesne, it is a salutary experience to stand on the motte of Farnham Castle and survey the fields below.

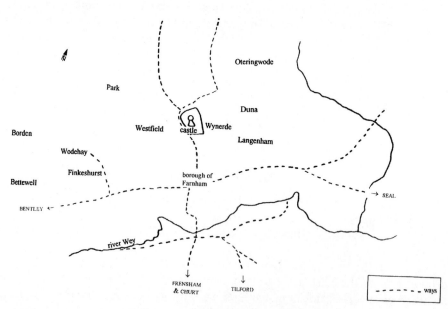

12: Farnham Manor Demesne Fields

There was the Wynerde (the field of the vineyard), and the Duna or Estdon; no longer names on a membrane but land once ploughed, sowed and reaped. One wonders how it was ever done with such poor equipment and

38

unwilling bondmen. It is difficult to imagine how anyone could have dreamed up the idea of calling the medieval period the era of High Farming.

Ploughing

The essential base for any good crop, garden or farm, is well cultivated ground. On the farm this meant starting with a well turned furrow of even width and depth. How near this ideal was attainable with the heavy wooden plough is a matter of speculation. Experience of ploughing heavy land in a wet season and downland in drought suggests not very near. Even with modern tractors, ploughing can be difficult on occasions. For example in the spring of 1947 a great deal of land was unploughable until late March, some because it remained frozen or snow-covered and some because the melting snow flooded it. The lack of a range of modern implements leads to the idea that corn had to be planted as soon as possible after ploughing in order to allow it to compete with weeds. That is practical common sense under the circumstances. It also may be the reason behind the phrase added to every definition of boon ploughing in the Farnham accounts: 'they shall plough 5 acres in autumn and 5 acres in spring with daily harrowing'. As these were customary acres the actual area ploughed was half a statute acre on each of the five days in spring and autumn for which they received ½d per day. If this is compared with a team of 1923 whose daily task was one acre, this appears to be realistic for what could have been done with a poor plough and ox team.

Harrowing

The term 'daily harrowing' is surprising. However it does seem to confirm the idea that corn had to be sown as soon after ploughing as possible. It would usually have been better, at least on heavy land, to leave it to weather a little. As they had no implement capable of dealing with emerging weeds, such as a cultivator or heavy harrow, they probably had no option. The act of harrowing is so simple that it might well be imagined that it would be easy to work out how and when it was done, the more so as in virtually every account there are references to harrowers, harrows, and horses for harrowing. However, despite examining many Farnham and Bentley accounts, no clear picture has emerged.

	Farnham	**Bentley**
1223	2 harrowers for 2 teams a carter who also did harrowing 1 harrower for half a year 1 harrower for 3 weeks	1 harrower for half a year
1225	2 harrowers for half a year	2 carters did the work
1231	shoeing one harrowing horse and 1 horse for the cart	

1245		1 harrower for 1 term (3 months)
		shoeing one harrowing horse
1246		1 harrower for 1 term
1251	1 harrower for 10 weeks	1 harrower for half a year

One could go on year after year with similar irregular entries. At this period the harrower was listed together with the reeve, ploughmen, shepherd, etc. in the Farnham account, so they were not casual workers. This changed in later accounts which did not include a harrower nor the corresponding quantity of grain usually issued to seasonal workers; it is tempting to suggest that as the harrowing did not require special skill it was done by anyone handy, just as in the 1920s. The one fact that does emerge, especially from the earliest figures, is that there was an awful lot of harrowing. In 1223 for instance about 140 acres of winter corn was sown. For this 2 men were harrowing for 3 months. In the following spring of 1224, 200 acres were planted and again there was 3 months' work for both men.

Seed Corn

The following figures[5] can be misleading unless it is recognised that the land is being measured in <u>customary</u> acres which in Farnham was about half a statute acre. It is easy to recognise the customary acre as the quantity of seed sown per acre is too low.

1223

Seed	Acreage#	Demense	Total Quantity	Bushels/ Acre
rye	64	Farnham	10½ qtr	1.3*
barley	27	Farnham	12 qtr 2 bushels	2.4*
	14	Sele		
oats	372	Farnham		
	87	Sele	177 qtr	2.8*
	28	Frensham[6]		

#In addition circa 300 acres would have been fallow   **calculated*

Except under special circumstances the seed rate of 2½ bushels per statute acre for winter corn and of 4 bushels per statute acre for spring corn has remained constant down to the present day. In many of the later accounts, the actual seed rate was recorded together with the total used.

1300–1301

Seed	Acreage	Demense	Quantity	Bushels/ Acre
wheat	31	West field		2½
winter barley	4	West field	1 qtr 4 bushels	3
spring barley	10	Wynerd	5 qtr 3 bushels	4 plus 2 pecks
oats	33	Wynerd and Medmulle[7]	20 qtr 7 bushels	5 plus 2 pecks

When the acreage does not divide exactly into the quantity of grain, the surplus was carefully noted. This suggests that they were quite happy to allow a little for spillage etc rather than be short of grain for the last odd corner at the end of the day.

It is difficult to get any idea of the quality of the seed. It would be easier to discuss yields if there was knowledge of what it would have produced under modern experimental conditions. Despite this there is no doubt that it was incapable of yielding anything like that obtained in the 1920s. This is shown by the need of farmers in the 17th and 18th centuries to find better strains. One suspects that the quality of the seed had more effect on yield than is generally recognised. On the other hand it can be argued that conditions were often so unfavourable that even better seed would have fared as badly. One fact worth noting is the similarity of the medieval seed rate to the modern one. This can be useful where medieval figures are suspect. Titow and others have noted that there were sometimes sudden increases. The obvious reason, though not necessarily the right one, is dubious seed. During a wet harvest, grain often sprouts in the ear. If too far gone, it will not thresh. If the germ is just alerted but has not emerged and the weather turns hot and dry, the grain may thresh in due course. In that case the seed might be a mixture of live and dead grains and it would therefore have been prudent to increase the seed rate substantially.

The Seed Bed

Few people today know that the seed bed required for broadcast corn differs from that for drilled corn, the advantage of the latter being that it places the seed in rows at a pre-determined depth. Rows were an improvement as they made subsequent weeding with hoe or spud easier. Sowing at a pre-determined depth was more important as it solved a major problem – irregular germination. When broadcast, the grain lies on the surface of the ground. It is then at the mercy of birds; flocks of house-sparrows, pigeons, rooks etc can clear uncovered grain in hours. The seed therefore has to be covered immediately. When seed is broadcast on ground prepared by modern harrows the tine indentations leave grooves into which the grain can be pushed by a following harrow. When I broadcast seed during the last war, it came up in regular lines.

The medieval farmer did not, indeed could not produce a surface as regular as can be made today. He therefore had a bed whose irregularities left cavities for the seed. After the seed was broadcast, which is relatively quick and accurate, the surface was harrowed. For this a brush harrow was used. It has already been described how there must always have been quantities of weed trash to dispose of. Even with modern implements it is difficult to remove or bury weeds completely, and unrotted matter often comes up again in subsequent cultivations. The medieval light or even heavy tined harrow would have been little use as tines would block or ride over bunched trash leaving uncovered grain. These problems were solved by using a harrow which brushed soil over grain lying in indentations on the surface, whilst at the same time riding over trash without collecting it up in heaps. The brush harrow consisted of a wooden frame into which were thrust branches of hawthorn or blackthorn so that they protruded four or five feet beyond the back of the frame. It was easy to repair on the spot. If more weight was needed a log could be put on top. I saw a brush harrow made using a gate for the frame on Yates Farm, Wigston Fields in Leicester in 1921 or 1922. Brush harrowing is referred to in a number of the Bentley manor accounts in the last years of the 13th century and the early ones of the 14th, 6/9d being paid in lieu of doing brush harrowing as bondwork. The account for 1318[8] is more informative:– '6/9d (in lieu) of dusteggyng from 40 bondmen of the lord holding 20 virgates this year'.

Broadcasting corn had one enormous disadvantage which may have caused, and almost certainly did cause bad harvests of spring-sown corn. When there is a dry spring or even a normal one with a dry spell, corn lying within the top half an inch or less of soil will not germinate, or if it germinates will fail to thrive. In these conditions being near the surface it was liable to damage from birds. Equally bad was irregular germination. On damper areas, germination might be normal whilst adjacent seed could lie dormant for days. This was one of the fatal disadvantages of the ridge and furrow lands. One year in the early 1980s, spring corn sown on ploughed-out ridge and furrow failed entirely on one field. On another it germinated slowly in the remains of the furrows and weeks later on the crests of the old ridges. I have seen the same occurring on old downland. This problem was later solved by rolling the seed bed after sowing and harrowing. It brought up moisture, just as a brick does if left on the ground. It was not a problem with autumn corn as the seed bed could be rougher without disadvantage since clods weathered down in the winter.

Hazards

When brush harrowing was done, sowing was finished. The time between sowing and harvest is not without hazards. Searing spring winds can damage winter corn under extreme conditions, the more so if they come late after a mild winter and growth is sappy. A more important hazard is the attack on the growing corn by wireworm, slugs, and leatherjackets. By the end of April or early May weeds will be advanced. In the 1920s thistles were spudded as the hoe is of little use in corn, and docks were dug with a narrow two-tined fork so as not to disturb the corn. The dock roots were put in a bucket and thrown onto the hedge at the side of the field. It was a cold tedious job, even more so for a boy on his own day after day, as was usually the case. My diary for 1928 reads:

Monday 7th May Started docking in the Open Close with Tidman and Fred.
Wednesday 28th May Very cold and wet all day. Finished docking.

Little or nothing can be done with spring-germinating weeds. In every early Pipe Roll account, there is recorded the payment for bondwork of weeding the corn – it may have been done and paid for but there was no guarantee that it was properly done. Weeding has never been a popular job with the corn often wet and spring days not always radiant. It is easy to blur the work so that it looks good, but the weeds are not properly severed, or are left with a fragment of root attached. Weeding on the demesne by unwilling bondmen is unlikely to have done more than check the weeds, giving the growing corn a little more space and light; thistles always sprout a second time. How much the growing corn suffered from pests destroying stem or ear is unknown. It is difficult to imagine that it was immune.

In July the principal hazard would have been laid corn. This was always a problem with the former taller varieties. Wind and rain can sweep across a field and lay acres in an hour or two. If laid in the early summer, most of the corn would be lost since it will either fail to ripen or be taken by the birds, for them a special feast! In the 1920s with a binder it was an awful nuisance. Reaped by hand, more was likely to be saved; the more so if it was nearly ripe before going down. One wonders whether the crops of thistle compensated by holding up the corn ... but if you have worked in such a field you would not think anything could compensate for raw arms at the end of the day.

Harvest

The harvest was not free from hazards. Once the corn was reaped and tied by straws into sheaves it had to be left in the field to dry. By custom on the Frensham Beale manor, according to depositions given in the tithe case of circa 1790, wheat was stooked in tens so that tithes could be collected easily. When the taking of tithes in kind was abandoned, eight or ten sheaves continued as it was the number that would dry best without collapsing. Wheat had to be left out 15 days or more, but if completely dry with the grain hard it could be carted and stacked when damp with water running out of the wagons as the saying was. In that condition it could not be threshed until it had dried out, sometime after Christmas. Oats, sometimes reaped with green tinged straw, had to stay out three weeks to avoid moulding in the stack.

During these periods in the field, the crop was open to inclement weather, birds, particularly rooks and pigeons, and man. Not for nothing was a watchman paid for nights in the field 'at the time of harvest'. Once stacked, the corn was safe – except from rats and mice in their thousands. And of course trouble when violent storms tore the thatch off as it often did to the farm buildings by the Castle.

Perhaps the reader might think that there was quite enough described already to make any likelihood of corn-filled barns remote. But he would be wrong, there was still one more hindrance. No harvest work was done on a Sunday. I have memories of walking amongst the stooks in blazing heat on a Sunday, only to wake next day to see dripping trees and drowned fields – and a spoilt harvest.

Notes

[1] One has little confidence in a writer who suggested feeding wheat straw, which is virtually inedible, to animals.

[2] This was possible from the writer's experience of working on farms in the late 1920s, in particular from a diary kept from August 1926 to August 1929. This included a year on a large mixed farm at Shilton, Warwickshire, then considered one of the best managed in the Midlands. Although on somewhat different soil, the implements and cultivations would have been similar to those necessary at Farnham in 1923.

[3] *Pipe Roll B1/10 159278*

[4] 5 bigas paid for bringing salt from Bitterne to Farnham 10/- *Pipe Roll B1/10 159278*

[5] To digress slightly, these figures are adequate to give an idea of what the demesne was in 1223 but it cannot be emphasised enough how important it is not to use such figures out of context. To quote Miss Cash who was County Archivist at the Hampshire Record Office when I was reading the Pipe Rolls "I don't want to know what it says, I want to know what it means!" To achieve this would require a complete translation of all the Rolls.

[6] This land, previously been held by the Dammartins who had large estates elsewhere, was farmed by the demense until it was handed over to tenants in 1231 and 1232.

[7] circa 2 acres

[8] Ref: B1/74 159333

Farming in Churt

As far as can be seen from the Pipe Rolls, by the early 14th century Churt had become a fairly stable community of small farms. What were these farms like? Although small by modern standards they were not so by comparison with farms in other tithings of Farnham. If taxation is a measure of prosperity, the sums levied from tenants in 1332[1] even suggest that Churt was one of the more prosperous tithings. Only rarely did any bondman have more than one virgate[2], explicitly stated in the Pipe Rolls to be 32 statute acres in Farnham manor. Most Churt farms were a whole or a half virgate. From the crop yields on the demesne, especially from Seale whose light soil was similar to that of Churt, it is possible to calculate what farms could produce. If one discounts unploughable land, and every virgate must have had some, the optimum area of arable land would have been about 24 – 25 acres. With the then current three-course rotation of winter corn, spring corn and fallow, average yields, calculated from figures for Farnham demesne 1340–1349, would have been about:

Oats	spring sown	3 cwt per acre	=	24 cwt
Wheat	winter sown	6¼ cwt per acre	=	50 cwt

It is unlikely that much wheat was grown in Churt as the soil is too light. Like Seale, rye was preferred. Though the yields quoted are averaged, they were rarely exceeded. They are 'averages' in a farming sense, not mathematical ones. The yields that exceeded the nominal mean never compensated for those that were below. Average in a farming sense means a yield that could reasonably be hoped for. It was rarely achieved.

These figures are put in perspective by the quantities of corn[3] issued to workers on the demesne in addition to cash wages. The standard amount was 6½ quarters per year, extra for the more important people, the hayward etc., and less for casual workers. Whatever the amount, it was calculated exactly according to the time worked. During the 13th century it was usually wheat, rye, or mancorn (mixed wheat and rye), later more often oats or barley. Whatever the grain, the quantity never changed. If the basic allowance of

45

about 27 cwt is set against the yield of 50 cwt, and 11 cwt is deducted for seed, it can be seen that only in good years would the theoretical virgate produce much surplus. If one considers further that half the land holdings in the whole manor were half virgates, it is easy to understand why people starved in bad years.

These calculations are made on the assumption that most of the land was under arable cultivation. There is evidence that some land was wooded. When the bishop required two oak beams for the boat being built at Southwark in 1310, he had it selected 'from the woods of John de Hide'. Some three hundred years later in 1640 the jury of Churt presented John Bristowe for making waste of wood and timber trees on the land of the heir of Richard Upfold, he being an infant'[4]. There is also the practical side: how much was the 13th century family capable of cultivating? And finally motivation. Except perhaps in times of great prosperity, it was axiomatic that the smaller and poorer farms nearly always had the worst farmers to manage them. One only needs to read the various surveys of England made during the 18th and 19th centuries to see how true that was.

Arable cultivation beyond what could be done by hand depended on animal motive power; so what animals did the virgators have? Until the end of the 17th century, and in most places even later, wintering of bovines was limited by the amount of hay that could be made. In mild winters some use could be made of rough grazing. Oat straw was also used to some extent. The hard fact remained, as clearly shown on the demesne farm at the castle, that wintering livestock was a precarious business.

In Churt it may have been even more difficult as there were only small patches of meadow hay land. It also has to be remembered that although the accounts of the demesne farm at the castle are the yardstick against which these assumptions are measured, the resources it commanded were infinitely superior. Even though large parts of the Farnham hay meadows belonged to the demesne, the oxen usually required winter feeding with barley or oats. Given the grain yields in Churt and the size of the farms, there would have been little to spare for oxen in a bad winter. From the evidence in my possession, it would seem that the Churt virgators before 1348 maintained oxen and other livestock, much as is factually recorded in the late 16th century Headley inventories (see later in this chapter).

Weeds

It is necessary to describe some of the limitations and difficulties faced by early Churt farmers. In particular we may not know with certainty how they behaved when faced with weeds, but we do know how weeds behaved to them.

The average yield of wheat on the Castle demesne farm at Farnham 1315 to 1339 inclusive was 5 cwt per acre. During the first nine years it failed to reach 4½ cwt (1 qtr). These figures probably convey little to most readers. Compared to yields in the 1920s they look exceedingly odd when the average

46

national yield was 15 cwt per acre, three times the medieval. This may not cause surprise unless it is complemented with the fact that in the 1920s any crop which looked like yielding much less than 7 or 8 cwt would have been ploughed up. It would have been so thin that weeds would have smothered what was left. Put trenchantly, the medieval crop was at best about half the worst crop grown in 1920. These figures are facts, how can they be explained? The answer is, with difficulty, although it certainly includes factors described below.

The plants which invade cultivated land are too numerous to mention here. Some are almost universal, others restricted to particular soils. For practical purposes they divide into two classes, high growing and creeping. The old farming methods could check both types but never eradicate them. Poppies, charlock, thistles and fat hen were typically high-growing weeds. The thistle excepted, they produced millions of seeds with the property of being able to lie dormant in the soil for more years than is known. Reaping corn thick with charlock was like cutting gooseberry bushes. Carts at the end of the day could be deep in charlock or poppy seed shed from the sheaves. Although both would germinate at any time, they were typically spring weeds. Thistles hardly need describing, though the sight of acres of thistley corn, mauve in the sun is now rarely seen.

Of the many creeping weeds, only couch requires description. Left alone it spreads with speed on any soil, its most troublesome property being the ability to grow from any fragment. This meant that cultivations could even encourage its spread. Several methods of control were later devised. In a dry spring, land could be pared and burnt. A better way was to plough a couchy fallow once every month from April to September. This worked fairly well, but depended on perfect ploughing, so as to leave the weed completely buried each time. Paring and burning was done in the Middle Ages; however it was labour-intensive. It only works well in a dry spring and would be of limited use except on small areas or where labour was cheap and abundant. One is bound to ponder, not that their crops were poor, but that they grew anything at all.

Traditionally the fallow was ploughed twice before the winter corn was sown. The records for Farnham exhibit that this was not always possible. Ploughing was done in the spring after the fallows had been grazed. The idea that animals returned significant fertility to the land[5] is a misconception, and generally the effects of this grazing are misunderstood; it probably, almost certainly, had another purpose. Although pictures of medieval reaping usually show clean cutting near ground level, it wasn't done like that in Farnham. Most of the early 13th century farm buildings in the outer court of Farnham Castle were thatched. For this the corn stubble and weeds were cut after the grain has been reaped. Straw for thatching was then extracted and put into heaps, the actual number of heaps being recorded. The Frensham Beale manor account of 1346 also gives an idea of what the land was like after the harvest: '10½d paid to a man mowing the stubble for forage'. The fact that is was worth mowing indicates beyond doubt that the corn had been full of grass and weeds at harvest. The grazing of fallow was therefore not only a minor source of food for livestock but also the only way of breaking up the post-harvest rubbish so that it could be buried in a narrow furrow. If one pictures docks, couch and thistles four feet high in the corn, the problem begins to take shape. It is usually forgotten that corn was formerly much longer in the straw, drawing up weeds growing amongst it. If this trash could not be reduced to fragments between harvest and spring corn or during fallow, a good seed bed was impossible. This alone could account for the miserable yields of medieval crops, without all the other hazards.

Looked at from the distance of centuries, it is impossible to avoid posing the question, 'Why did they not grow less acreage and cultivate it better?' In theory at least, five acres of weed-free corn would have yielded more than ten of the then current demesne acres, and that area could have been dealt with easily. The people were not stupid. One can only suppose that there was some factor that has hitherto escaped notice. The relative inefficiency of their ploughs has already been noted. Harrows being furnished with wooden tines could not have been very effective on stiff ground. Above all they lacked a tool like a modern cultivator which could turn up young weeds at a pace three or four times faster than the plough.

The Cropping

Despite the difference in time, the inventories of some Headley farmers in the sixteenth century provide the best clues for farming in Churt before the Black Death. It has been said that they are unrepresentative as they only record the assets of older men whose farms may have run down, but this is not so. As the wills show, quite a number died suddenly or young. There seems little doubt that if one takes the pre-1600 inventories, excluding one or two known to be of richer farmers on better land, the remainder represent farming similar to that in the first half of the 14th century. Techniques of farming had not changed much, because before the Tudors there was nothing to cause it to do so.

Although there is no specific evidence concerning ploughing in Churt and Headley, the Pipe Rolls provide evidence of arable work on the demesne lands of Farnham, Bentley, and Frensham Beale manors, and of Seale. Although it may appear simple to deduce what took place, crude calculations can be hopelessly misleading. Apart from lack of descriptive content to show how the acres were actually ploughed – and even the number of oxen used in a team, and the ploughs available – there is a factor usually neglected, time. Whatever figures suggest, the work had to fit in with days available in autumn and spring, particularly the latter. The key figures are those for the spring. The possible sowing time started from about mid-February lasting to mid-April. Sowing before mid-February must have been rarely possible, or desirable. Sowing after mid-April acquired the name of 'cuckoo corn', each day later significantly decreasing the yield. If one excludes the average number of days lost through inclement weather, Sundays and Easter, possible sowing days are considerably reduced.

In theory, and often no doubt in practice, the standard team was made up of eight oxen. If the crude Farnham figures are used, it can be seen that 8 or 9 teams could have ploughed the area available for sowing within the time limit. Practical considerations, such as not all the oxen being fit to work for some or all of the time, and/or if the weather was bad, would have made it impossible. This is probably what is reflected in the actual acreages planted. Although the size of the individual fields remained constant, the areas planted varied from year to year. The figures for Bentley over the same period of 1215 to 1350 show the effect of the land there being heavier than at Farnham.

Frensham manor was in the hands of the bishop during 1242–1247. The land there is mostly lighter land than at Farnham and rather similar to that at Seale and Churt. One of the oddites at Frensham was the irregularity of the areas of winter and spring corn sowed. In 1242 for instance, 20½ acres of winter corn was sown as against 60 acres of oats. The number of oxen in each year was 5 or 6, (depending if one was sold and another bought), with three plough horses. Calculated on the same basis as Farnham, the single team could not in any way have completed its task. There has to be some explanation. The obvious one, to anyone who has not seen the original documents, is that ploughs and teams were hired to complete the work. In fact this was rarely done, and in each case, the cost and an explanation was given; shortage of labour or extra land taken on being the usual reasons. The Frensham solution lies in the fact that though the eight-ox team was not only usual but necessary on heavy or moderately heavy land, it was not so on the light land in parts of West Surrey. The task at Frensham manor could only have been completed if their oxen and horses were split into two or three teams. Support for this idea is contained in the Headley inventories. These show that out of 107 farms only eight had as many as six oxen, four of which were special cases (see below).

Inventories

On the basis of the foregoing, Churt farms before the Black Death had few bovines, and rarely more than a couple of horses, one of which was often a foal, as can be seen in the following inventories of Hugh of Overton and John of Thone. Though apparently little more than curiosities, these two inventories, when compared with those of the sixteenth century, provide useful clues to the pre-1348 farming. In or about 1251 there was a considerable 'commotion' at Farnham. People were killed, hung, or fled. Nothing is known of the cause or how many were involved. Only the names of the major participants or victims remain. Amongst those who fled the manor was Hugh of Overton. His livestock, forfeited to the bishop, was: half a young horse[6], 6 ewes, 41 wethers, 24 hoggs[7], 4 lambs. As the sheep were described as 'after shearing', the actual date was therefore June-July 1252. In 1268, John de la Thone was hung at Winchester. His possessions were: half a young horse, 1 plough horse, 2 cows with calves, 3 young steers, 10 ewes, 22 wethers, 18 lambs, and corn worth 26/8d.

The parish of Headley, Churt's neighbour to the west, has a good collection of inventories and wills for the period 1551 to 1641. These describe farming much as would be expected as customs and general management of the land changed little over centuries having evolved from what had been found most suitable.

Headley Inventories

Period	No. of inventories	No. with ploughs	No. with oxen	No. of oxen on individual farms		
1551 – 1569	19*	3	5	6, 6, 6	4, 4	2
1570 – 1578	17**	6	7		4, 4	2, 2, 2
1579 – 1592	20	6	11	6, 6, 6	4, 4	2, 2, 2, 2, 2, 2
1597 – 1615	17	6†	7	6	4, 4, 4	2, 2, 2
1616 – 1632	19	7	6	5	4, 4, 3	2, 2
1632 – 1641	15	5††	9	6	4, 4, 4, 4	2, 2, 2, 2
Totals:	107	34	45			

Note: Most of the farms with 4 or 6 oxen were on better land beyond the boundaries of the Bargate beds.

* 5 had no corn, including a fuller and a weaver
** 2 had no corn
† plus 1 wheat plough
†† 3 of the 5 had more than one plough

Most farmers were slow to change until a neighbour's crops were either new or more profitable. That is why the earlier inventories up to about 1590 are probably not much out of line with what was done before 1348, except in one thing, scale. The Tudor farms were two virgates or sixty acres, double the size of the medieval farms. There was also a social change. The medieval virgate had been, as far as can be judged, worked by an extended family. The Tudor farms used the same labour in numbers but there was a change to farmer and paid workers. Evidence though uncertain and fragmentary points to the population remaining much the same. A more significant change in the long run was the advent of landlord and tenant farming. Before 1348, the bishopric had been strict concerning sub-lettings. Licences were rarely granted, only one or two before 1348, and penalties were severe: three tenants of Tilford were heavily fined for letting land to

Waverley Abbey. The fine books for the Tudor period are sprinkled with such licences being granted by the bishop. Most of the new landlords were local business people, the Mantes and the Paines being good examples.

The most interesting information in the inventories concerns the scale of arable farming. They show that although corn was grown on nearly every farm, only half had ploughs and oxen, not entirely surprising when seen in the context of the Farnham demesne farm, where oxen often had to be fed corn in the winter, died of weakness, 'debilitate', or were sold for their hides. The smaller farmer could neither afford to feed oxen, nor run the risk of a good ox in the autumn being a dead one in the spring, or without sufficient strength to do useful work. Either way, he was the loser. Although there is no direct evidence, one supposes that ploughing was done for neighbours on some basis, like "I'll plough for you, you help with my harvest".

Sheep numbers fluctuated with prices. Cattle and pig numbers remained stable as only a certain number could be fed. Corn prices fluctuated, sometimes wildly, but it seems unlikely that this affected the acreage grown, at least in the short term. Before 1600 the major crops were rye and oats. Little wheat was grown in Headley (or Churt), the land being too light to produce good crops even today with fertiliser and better varieties.

From the inventory dated 17 April 1566 of Robert Harding who lived at Plaster Hill, west of Barford:

20 ewes	1 horse
14 lambs	2 acres of rye, 3 of oats, in the ground
48 teggs or wethers	1 cock and 6 hens

He lived in an open hall house which preceded the present one built by his descendants. His land which lay on the south side of the Headley Lane was described in the 1552 Parliamentary Survey as 24 acres comprising: 5 closes, 11 acres; 3 closes, 9 acres; a grove of 4 acres; Rent 6/8: suit of court money 7d. He also had one little close of ½ acre and 16 acres in 3 closes: Rent 7/8.

Taken from the inventory of William Luffe of Hide who died in the spring of 1582 (no precise date):

6 cows, 1 bull	168 sheep	cocks, hens and ducks
4 oxen	26 lambs	4 pigs
1 steer	3 mares	Rye in the field 47/8
6 bullocks	1 gelding	Lenten (spring) tillage £5.5.0
3 calves	1 foal	

Differences in valuations given in inventories can be great, reflecting the date[8] of valuation and the state of the crops, and make it impossible to calculate the acreage of the corn. From the valuation in William Luffe's inventory a wild guess would be 10 acres of rye and 20 acres of oats, rather more than less, which would appear to make Hide a big farm or the biggest in Churt – exactly what could be expected from other evidence. The land described in the fine of 1503 shows that it consisted of three virgates, previously single farms, an outlier of 17 acres at Greencross and another 10 to 15 acres of oddments. This is roughly the size of four pre-1348 Churt farms. If one divides Luffe's crops and animals by four the resulting portions are each surprisingly similar to those of Hugh of Overton of 1251, John de la Thone of 1268, and Robert Harding of 1566. Further, if the inventories of Hugh of Overton and John of Thone, with a few personal items added, were accidentally set beside Robert Harding's inventory, it would escape notice that their dates are a few hundred years apart. It seems reasonable to state that the external pressures on Churt farms were much the same in the 16th century as in the 13th century.

The cumulative evidence points to Churt before the Black Death being a district of small farms, producing enough for a family, even an extended one, to be nearly self-sufficient. In most years there was a surplus sufficient to pay taxes and necessary purchases but it was never very much. In good years, prices dropped, in bad years they rose; that helped little as there was less to eat and nothing to sell. It seems a dubious existence, eased, if the Perquisites of the Court are to be believed, by considerable quantities of ale; but they were better off than their forebears a few generations earlier who had been bondmen of the lord and little more than slaves. Everything points to the pre-1348 farms being a desperate fight for survival. Crops at the mercy of weeds, weather, birds, wild animals, and livestock, subject to all the ills faithfully recorded on the Pipe Rolls of murrain, scabiosa, and starvation. Given that land, weeds, climate, and probably human nature were the same, it seems likely that the 13th and 14th century Churt farms were much the same as those of the 16th century.

Notes

[1] Appendix: lay subsidy for Churt 1332

[2] See P D Brooks, *The Bishop's Tenants*

[3] As the corn was measured by volume, the bondman did best with wheat, less well with barley and badly with oats: wheat 4½cwts per qrt; barley 4 cwts per qrt; oats 3 cwts per qrt. The food value of wheat or rye was slightly better than barley and much better than oats.

[4] Consistory Court Rolls, 155/5, HRO

[5] This was true of the later period when animals were hard folded on root crops.

[6] The shared animal was common; where half an animal was forfeit or due as a heriot, the bishop bought the other half.

[7] Male sheep up to 1 year old

[8] After about 1560, corn prices dropped sharply; but there are not enough examples to press the point.

The Manor of the Bishop

In 688 Caedwalla, King of the South Saxons, made a grant of 60 hides of land for the foundation of a church at Farnham, two hides of which were in Churt. It was from this grant that the great manor of Farnham, held by the bishopric of Winchester, evolved.

It is a popular misconception that the bishops of Winchester owned their various manors; they did not. The bishopric alone owned them and individual bishops were simply life tenants. Each one had to settle with his predecessor's executors or bishopric officials, as did his own executors in turn. Every inhabitant of Farnham manor was also a tenant of the current bishop, and indirectly of the bishopric, which owned everything on the manor and the soil beneath it. The bishop's riches, and they were great, derived from the profits of the manor, from minerals, timber, crops, fisheries, and everything large and small that could be produced, consumed, or sold. Originally the bishop's farms in the manor, the demesne, had been cultivated by tenants bound to the manor, not free to leave or marry without permission. By the early 13th century this system was breaking down in Farnham and many tenants were already paying rent by a combination of money and work service. The change to money rent alone was early in Farnham – the process is too complicated to describe here, but has been written up elsewhere[1].

The whole manor was split up into a number of tithings, each being an individual administrative area. The tithing of Churt which included Pitfold (now Shottermill) stretched from Frensham Pond to the border with Sussex. Each tithing had a tithingman whose duties, never commented on in the Rolls, included reporting local matters at the manor court; he had little real power. In early accounts he was often amerced singly or together with the whole tithing for failing to perform some duty. One failed to report that the men of Elstead had killed and eaten a stray horse; all of Churt was fined for failing to keep and produce a malefactor before the Court[2].

When a tenant acquired land, an entry was made in the Farnham account on the Pipe Roll. The final accounts were compiled at Wolvesey, the bishop's palace at Winchester, from material supplied by the officials at Farnham.

These entries which came to be called 'fines of land' were in effect registrations of title, for which an entry fine had to be paid[3]. There were several different kinds of land and these were reflected in the wording of the fines. Land which had formerly paid rent in work service was described as bondland, and the rent for this was paid at Michaelmas, Christmas, Easter and Hockday. Land taken out of 'the waste of the lord' was described as 'purpresture' and the rent for this was paid at Michaelmas and Easter. When such land was first taken from the waste, two entries were made in the account for that year: the first at the head of the account was the 'New rent'[4] and the second was the entry fine which appeared under 'Fines and marriages'.

There was also a small amount of free land usually held by tenants of higher social standing. Land was only free in the sense that no obligation for work service was attached to it. On entry a 'relief' was paid: in theory a voluntary contribution, which in practice was obligatory.

Rent once fixed could not be altered; fines on the other hand could be. Some entry fines continued unaltered for many years whilst others changed. For example when a widow inherited a life interest, the fine was reduced; other alterations were for reasons which we do not understand. The early 13th century fines were mostly for land ascribed to a single name such as John, William etc. After the middle of the 13th century the entries became more informative. Of particular importance are those fines which not only located the land in a particular tithing, but also added a descriptive note, 'in the marsh', 'on better land', 'together with grass [hay] on it', etc. From these later fines a picture evolves of land and land holding in Churt and the other tithings in the manor of Farnham.

Notes

[1] *Surrey Archaeological Collections* Vol. 85 1998: Farnham town, borough and manor in the early 13th century by P D Brooks

[2] The Consistory Court Rolls 16th to 18th century deposited at HRO contain some interesting comments and notes from Churt tithingmen. The Paine / Mantle case documents 1780–1800 deposited at GMR also throw light on the tithingman's troubles in Farnham.

[3] See examples of fines for Churt in Manorial Fines chapter.

[4] for assarts or new land

High Churt

The eastern part of Churt contains the best farming land in the present parish. The name of High Churt covered the land between Hale House Lane and Green Lane, and from the tithing and parish boundary in the east to the ridge on the west of the Tilford road (Fig 13).

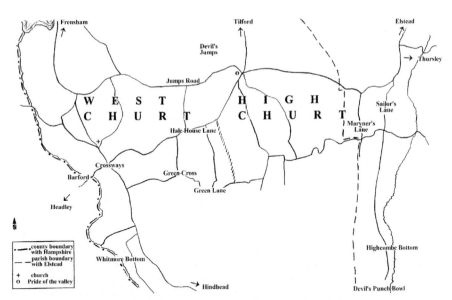

13: Churt divided into 'West Churt' and 'High Churt'

The three roads in this area and the dividing hedge lines between them show by their wandering nature that they are old. It can be divided into six nearly equal pieces laid out on a north-south axis, each pair of plots having until recently, a central road. Compared with the remainder of Churt and with Headley manor, it is apparent that High Churt derived from a definite plan (Fig 14) and not from random clearing of former waste.

55

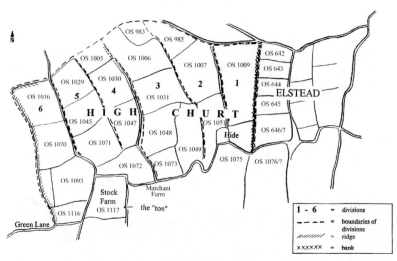

14: Planned divisions of High Churt

It is said that there is no record of Roman remains in Churt. However, with known Roman occupation only a few miles away at Frensham it is unlikely that the north slopes of Hindhead were untouched, particularly at High Churt which was on a substantial area of easily worked land; one might at least expect that there would have been a Romano-British farm such as has been discovered at Frensham Manor, or even earlier occupation. It would be prudent to look for pottery remains when opportunity arises.

The value of land to the Saxon bishopric of Winchester derived from what it could produce from farming and natural products. The question therefore arises – was the regular plan of High Churt the result of Saxon farming or from the Norman succession? It is easy to forget that the Saxon period lasted about 600 years, long enough for land to be cleared, go back to waste and be cleared again, none of which would be apparent a thousand years later. Schoolchildren used to be taught about the Normans taking over Saxon-held land (in much the same way as the Saxons were supposed to have displaced the Britons). Although undoubtedly Saxon nobles and landholders were replaced by Normans, it would not have been the same with the peasantry. The incoming Normans were not so devoid of common sense as to drive away the very people they needed to work the land they had acquired. No doubt there was some local rough and tumble, but it is unlikely that there was much change for ploughman or shepherd[1]. On this basis one might reasonably suggest that High Churt had a Saxon origin, and continued unaltered (or little altered) by the Norman bishops. The slowness of change is emphasized by the continued use of the Saxon or customary acre well into the 13th century. To anyone with memories of the old farming this would seem unsurprising. As long as the Saxon peasantry did their daily stint of ploughing and reaping, it did not matter how the 'acre' was measured, only the corn in the grange was important.

The farmlands at Bentley, Farnham, and Seale were situated around roughly central cores of granges etc. This was impossible at Churt owing to the narrowness of the Bargate Beds, land division being practical only on a north-south axis. How fast or slowly the plan of High Churt developed is unknown. Like the Midland ridge and furrow lands it could hardly have been done in a short period. The final result was three fields side by side, the field on the east bounding with the tithing of Elstead (or what became Elstead), and that on the west respecting a natural ridge, turning neatly on the crest of a hill at the north-west corner (*Fig 15*).

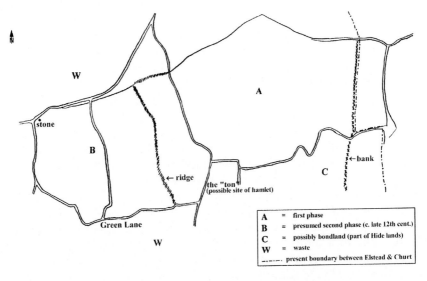

15: Phases of bondland development in High Churt

Each field was very roughly 60 statute acres, divided into two equal parts by a central road. The Hide road is now obliterated, the Marchants Farm road blocked and only the Tilford–Hindhead road remains. Although they now look like typical rural lanes, there is little doubt that they started as plough headlands and became roads from carrying produce between field and farm buildings. They also provided access for the flocks of sheep between the upper and lower commons. What remain today are only the traces of the final extent – or perhaps more accurately the greatest extent – of bishopric farming in Churt. If it were not for the Pipe Rolls that would be the sum of our knowledge.

During the first three decades of the 13th century, farming on the demesne reached its peak. In the following three, owing to increase in population and difficulties with imposing bondwork, most of the demesne land was devolved to tenants, leaving only a relatively small mixed farm. This was better for all parties: the bishopric received a steady income from rents, in place of often miserable crop yields, and the bondman a small increase of independence. It is from the copious details of this demesne farming that something of what took place at Churt[2] can be deduced, though in one sense this is guesswork. Cropping however presents no difficulty. The soil was light, similar to that of Seale, and rye and oats were therefore the main crops, whereas wheat was of less importance than on the heavier land at Farnham. Barley and pulses (vetch, pea and bean) were grown from time to time but not regularly. The guess lies in the area cultivated. Even if the land was all cleared it does not follow that it was all cultivated each year. Nor is it known if the bondmen had plots or strips in the open fields.

During the 13th century there was a general scaling down of demesne farming over many parts of the country, which seems to have happened earlier in Farnham than in many other places. That there was trouble over the bondwork due on the Farnham demesne from the bondmen is evidenced in the surviving Pipe Rolls of 1231–1256. It is recorded in the account of 1247 that Churt paid 8/0d for six hides so that they could be free of bondwork. The bondworks in Farnham manor were finally commuted in 1256 for an annual payment from all the tenants. Following this commutation the Rolls contain regular recitals of what the tenants should do, and what they failed to do. They included a passage concerning Churt. Translated it reads (or implies) that the plough boons performed by tenants of the manor of Farnham were calculated on the basis of 32 hides, but they should not complain as it was really only 26 hides as Churt always paid 8/0d for six hides. This can be taken in several ways. It implies that Churt had long devolved to tenants and also that Churt was a precursor of the general devolution of land in Farnham. It supports, in a minor way, the idea that Churt had long been regarded as separate from the rest of the manor, derived perhaps from far-off days when the 2 hides of land in Churt had indeed been out by itself in the wilds.

If, as suggested, Churt had been something of a separate community two questions arise. Where did the peasants live, and why was no church erected? When the bishopric farm was at its peak a considerable number of people must have been employed either wholly or partly. They could have lived either on scattered holdings or on small pieces of land rendering seasonal bondwork as required. If one follows the old road, now the Green Lane, from Hide either on a map or on the ground to the western boundary of Marchants Farm, one finds that it makes four right angle turns before resuming its course to Barford and Headley. As no road or boundary turns or wanders without reason, it is a guess that the enclosed area of about 4 acres was once the site of the bondmen's hamlet (*Figs 14 & 15*). If this is correct, one wonders why Churt never acquired a church as Elstead and Seale did. The term 'High Churt'[3] may have derived from what seems to have been a folk memory of this settlement.

To the south of the Green Lane, the land is of of poor quality. The lane follows, for most of the way, the boundary between the Bargate and Hythe

Beds of the Lower Greensand; the latter is largely useless for agriculture. The name Poor Field illustrates this, as do the names given to fields by the late Lady Lloyd George, 'Faith, Hope and Charity'[4]; the first two apply in the spring and the last when contemplating the harvest. To the east including Marchants Farm all land on the south of the lane is poor, then that opposite Hide Farm and after Ridgeway Farm is better. The wandering boundary between OS 1075 and 1076, a continuation of the Hide eastern boundary, is certainly ancient. Fields OS 1076 and 1077 also look to have been part of the old Hide Farm; they are another part of the puzzle of the area around the Elstead – Churt boundary (*Fig 16*).

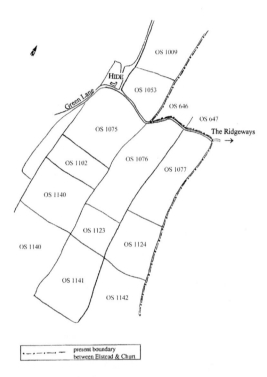

16: Boundary with Elstead at Hide farm

It is impossible to leave the land around the present boundary between Hide (Churt) and Elstead without identifying some of the problems thrown up by the Pipe Rolls and later documents. The most obvious problem is the position of this boundary in the 12th and early 13th centuries, which must have been a well-defined one or the respective tithingmen could not have performed their duties. It would be logical to suggest that any early boundary would have followed the course of one of the north-south crests or valleys, perhaps later masked by a road or track. Against such a background the right angle turn at Hide looks particularly odd. On the other hand, if one attempts to construct a boundary line from the evidence of the fines, not only the early fines but fines from as late as the 18th century, some places would be located on both sides of it. (Nor does it help to find that Wey Cottage[5] was held by the manor of Frensham Beale, as was Ridgeway Farm[6] if some 18th century documents are to be believed.) All one can do is to make a few guesses as to what may have been the cause of such confusion.

When and where was the first boundary between Churt and Elstead, and did the earliest scribes who compiled the bishopric accounts themselves know the exact geographical location of the places from which their revenues arose? It tends to be assumed that the accounts of the 1208 Pipe Roll are the first of the series, rather than the first to have survived. Given that, plus the fact that some fines contain inaccurate reading or copying of earlier ones by the scribes (eg Suttons by Somerset Bridge in Elstead appeared in the fines as Muttons for many years), there may be mistakes that are now unrecognisable as such. The taxation list of 1332[7] ought to have solved these problems, the more particularly as the order in which the names appear suggests that the collectors visited the farms in sequence: the last Elstead visit was to Crudescate and the next, the first of the Churt visits, was to Adam of Patifold at what is now Ridgeway. If this list is taken as a guide, all of what later became part of Elstead was then considered to be in Churt.

The three lanes that run north-south through the Hide lands occupy the sites of former plough headlands. The same applies to the long irregular hedge lines roughly parallel to them. The fields at the time of the tithe redemptions of 1832 had doubled in size by the time of the OS map of 1870. It now seems almost certain that these fields had already been enlarged during the fifty years prior to the date of the tithe survey. This was the best corn land in Churt and there would have been considerable pressure to remove any (by then) useless hedges. What remains today are mere fragments from a landscape of small fields whose origins lie in the medieval methods of cultivation.

It is seldom realised that the ancient open fields were not only split into large parcels for autumn corn, spring corn and fallow, but also into smaller areas within them. This was due to the nature of the plough and ploughing. When the plough is pulled across a slope it tends to slide downwards. This causes it to cut a wider furrow on one side and a narrower one on the other. It can be compensated for with a modern plough if the slope is not too great; however with the clumsier medieval one it could not. The land was therefore split up into sections so that it could be ploughed up and down to best advantage. Surviving ridge and furrow lands of the Midlands illustrate how it was done. Open fields subdivided in this way had two further advantages. It had long been discovered that oxen or other animals could do more work if rested from time to time, rather than in one continuous effort. For ploughing, the optimum distance was found to be about 200 yards. In time this became a recognised unit of length, the furrow long or furlong of 220 yards. Plough lands therefore tended to conform to slope and furlong where possible. The sub-areas of the open fields had another advantage. Medieval arable lands were almost unbelievably weedy by modern standards and it was therefore essential to sow seed immediately after ploughing. Weeds allowed to germinate or grow ahead of the corn always caused great difficulty and, in a wet year, disaster.

The acre evolved from the daily plough stint, no doubt a correct statement except for the fact that the acre concerned was the ancient customary or Saxon acre which is half the modern statute acre. If therefore a very long furrow had been ploughed, the area covered at the end of the day would have been only a narrow strip, not a useful plot. This is reflected in the plough boons described in the early Farnham Pipe Roll accounts. The daily work was one acre – one Saxon acre. Each statement, and there are many, ends with the words 'and daily harrowing'. Under normal conditions it would be wrong to harrow the furrows before they had weathered, unless the land was both light and dry. The medieval farmer had little option. He had neither time (especially in the Spring) nor implements with which to prepare a perfect seed bed. The shorter plough furrow length therefore was not only beneficial for the team, but gave a block of land rather than a strip for immediate sowing.

Once a field is ploughed traces of old furrows nearly always remain. Even with modern implements it is difficult to avoid leaving slight indent-ations. As many of the old fields tumbled down to grass, the furrows were seldom levelled and as a result old furrows survived for centuries. When the open fields of High Churt came to be ploughed again in the late 15th century, the old furrows and headlands were probably still visible. The new farmers re-used the old furrows as markers. As they were also starting to enclose small areas, it was natural to use the old headlands for new hedge lines. Any other line would have cut across actual or potential arable land. Of course there are variations. Physical features, and in places necessity for making small paddocks, would have interrupted the 'ideal' plan. Nevertheless this pattern can still be seen in many places where the old ridges and furrows still exist.

The same factors governed the enclosures of the western half of Churt (*Fig 17*), though not to the same extent. The longer hedge lines favoured the direction of the slope, but as the land had never been 'open' like Hide, enclosure was piecemeal. In High Churt, Outmoor for instance although probably cleared and enclosed piecemeal over a period, appears to have been within original fixed boundaries, which are now erosion banks on the south and west and roads on the east and north. On the other hand, the Barford lands west of the A287 are known to have been the result of steady encroachment into the waste in the late 12th and early 13th centuries. In all these cases it can be seen that the early bondmen had as good an eye for the land as some of their successors have today.

One corner of Churt has been the scene of several accidents. It is unlikely that the people involved ever knew that they took place on the site of a Saxon plough headland. I wonder if it was an echo of Saxon teams tangling in the same way. Traditionally the young ploughboy, learning his craft and put to easy harrowing, finished at least once with his horses on one side of a hedge and his harrow firmly anchored on the other!

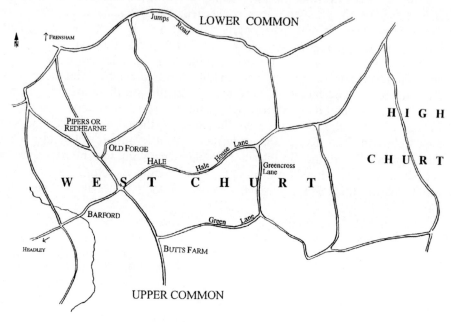

17: West Churt

As far as records allow it might be supposed that between the late 13th century and the Black Death in 1348, Churt experienced a period of stability. A closer look reveals a very different picture. It has long been established that after about 1300 there was a significant deterioration of climate which caused a series of disastrous harvests in the early years of the 14th century. Analysis of actual figures of corn yields in the manor of Farnham reveals that even in good years local produce barely covered local needs. Even allowing for inaccuracies of calculation or record it is clear that in many years there was an absolute shortage. The facts are confirmed in another way. For a separate purpose all the heriots paid on the deaths of head tenants have been extracted from the Pipe Rolls 1215–1349. The average per year was 7.6. In 1307 they rose to 22 and in 1311 and 1312, to 10 and 14 respectively. In 1325 they rose again to 14. The average of 7.6 heriots is compiled from figures that varied little from year to year, it is not a mean of extremes. Against this background the quoted totals show up dramatically. At the same time references began to appear for properties vacant or derelict, a fact confirmed by a lack of willing tenants. In the early years of the 13th century a new tenant was elected when there was a vacancy. After the bad years, election ceased and 'compulsis' entered the text. It reads as if a suitable person was told to look after the land, or else!

Although the 1332 taxation list suggests that Churt was still prosperous when compared with other tithings in the manor, the impression from reading all the accounts is that the bad years fatally damaged Churt's ability to recover quickly from the Black Death of 1348 and the plagues which followed.

1348–1500

The history of High Churt during these years can only be deduced from the fines, defaults of rent and a few field names, and so what follows here is necessarily unsatisfactory. In particular it lacks a first-hand, contemporary account of what the 'Great Pestilence' meant to one who had survived it. The cumulative effect of reading in account after account: 'derelict', 'lacking tenants for many years', 'no buyers' and similar phrases, is that Churt was a place of the doomed – which is almost certainly wrong.

From the earliest years there had been a section in the accounts headed 'Defaults of Rent'. In 1348 a new series was headed 'Defaults on account of the Pestilence'. As I began to look, very tentatively, at the accounts starting with the later ones of the 15th century, the full significance of this series was not understood until the Black Death defaults of 1348 and 1349 were translated. As a result only a few were included in notes. Nevertheless those produced here give a good idea of what they were like and more importantly, some definite information about the state of Churt before better years with the Tudors.

Date	Details	Rent Due	Rent Paid
1349	John Grover for ½ virgate	12/6	nil
	William Holonde for messuage, ½ virgate	4/2	nil
1350	William atte Holeland for messuage, ½ virgate	4/2	nil
1352	William atte Holeland for messuage, ½ virgate	3/8	6d

These are only a few of the defaults of which there was a long list every year. The defaults show that Churt was in such a state of decline that the inhabitants were, in most cases, only able to pay their rent in pence where formerly they had paid in shillings. At a very rough guess half the farms had near-destitute tenants surviving in decaying houses

It is usually supposed that the Black Death was a single great catastrophe. It was not, it was the forerunner of a series of plagues. A second outbreak in 1361 is considered to have mainly affected children. Another in 1396 is specially recorded in the Bentley account by the heading 'Magna Pestilencia', possibly made worse by the unusually wet summer when the corn was spoiled by a multitude of thistles making the harvest difficult and expensive

(Roll Year 1395–6). One result of the plagues was a change in the pattern of land transfer. Before 1348, except in rare cases, land was passed from father to son or, less often, to daughter or to widow. Even when this did not happen the inheritor was usually connected with the family in some way. In 1348 this pattern was broken. Between 1350 and 1399 there were 75 fines for Churt: of these only 19 showed inheritance from a parent. During the same time many new names appeared, some from other parts of the manor, others entirely new.

Another consequence of the plagues was the change in status of some families. This only becomes plain if the mass of later local documents are read. People whose names no longer appeared among landholders were not necessarily dead, they were 'broke'. Some farms disappeared from the records, only reappearing after about 1485. This may slightly overstate the case as there is evidence that some areas of the manor, including Churt, were occupied by farmers who leased the land without having a proper tenancy, and therefore no fines appeared in the accounts. Some credence is given to this by the change to farming out the flocks of sheep and herd of cows on the demesne farm in Farnham. Farmers leased flocks and herds, paying the bishop in cash and kind, having the profits for their management and work. By this time the hitherto large demesne had been reduced to that of a small-scale mixed farm. After the late 14th century the farmed-out herd of cows was only slightly increased, whereas flocks on the other hand increased to at least 500 wethers. These were the years when land was cheap and wool prices high, the years when great wool fortunes were amassed.

Enclosure of Fields

The date of the enclosure of the sub-division of the basic fields of High Churt with the lateral boundaries as demonstrated on Fig 14 is difficult to decide. Given the desire of tenants of the manor (and elsewhere) to obtain and enclose even the smallest piece of land to their own use and the record of Churt assarts, enclosure at an early date would seem to be most likely. The stark and cumulative record of decay in Churt after 1348 inhibits ideas of much improvement. One is therefore left with lateral enclosure of High Churt before 1348 or after mid-15th century. The problem is particularly difficult to solve as most of the hedges in east Churt have been obliterated. In west Churt, erosion banks are helpful since the hedges which caused them must be of considerable antiquity, whereas none of the existing lateral hedges in High Churt, nor the lines of missing hedges, show this to any degree. Only the deep erosions of the traversing and bisecting lanes derive with certainty from the old field system. In normal circumstances hedge vegetation would provide information. Unfortunately that which remains fails to conform to what has been found elsewhere, in addition to which the uncontrolled new growth since the last hedge maintenance in the 1920s–30s has obscured all but traces of what formerly existed. The regrowth of ash from old stumps is a useful clue. Luckily despite neglect and destruction, one hitherto unrecognised link with medieval Churt remains and this is the hedges consisting almost entirely of hazel. Except where obviously destroyed, they line nearly every road or lane in Churt. Hazel can certainly be found in a few lateral hedges, but only as an intruder. The assumption must be that the old open fields were divided by roads lined with hazel, and that the lateral divisions are products of a later period.

The fines of land after about mid-13th century invariably stated the size of the area involved, either by statute acre or perches and feet. Where it has been possible to identify them the measurements have been confirmed as accurate. It is likely that the three ten-acre plots of Robert Bat, Thomas Piper and John Foghell of 1419 were all measured and marked out at about the same time, and that the conformity of size was possible because the land was still open allowing unhindered measurement.

Date	Fine	Details	
1419	6d	John Foghell for a toft and 10 acres, once of Henry Heron	NS.[8]
1419	6d	Thomas Piper for 10 acres, once of Henry Heron	NS.
1419	6d	Robert Bat for 10 acres, once of Henry Heron	NS.

However, did Piper and his fellow tenants enclose their pieces out of the open field, or was it already enclosed? Other contemporary fines might have provided an answer. They do not, but they give a clue as to what the answer may be. Given the propensity for neighbours to quarrel over boundaries and the permutations of tenancy illustrated by the fines, it seems likely that boundaries not already in place were then being rapidly outlined.

The ten acre plots can hardly have been acquired for farming when large areas lay vacant and houses derelict. The particularly low fines being paid on entry to the land makes such an idea untenable. It is much more likely that cheap land was being bought as an investment, land being more secure than cash. If all the fines are examined it can be seen that this is exactly what was taking place. The stability of the pre-1348 years when everyone knew his place had given way to new people, short tenancies and secure boundaries. On present evidence High Churt was probably not fully enclosed from the open fields until the latter part of the 15th century.

Between 1348 and 1500 High Churt was only part occupied and farmed. There is certainly nothing to indicate any real farming, nor is there evidence of flocks from outside randomly grazing the commons. There was plenty of time for good oaks to have grown, and nothing in later years to suggest that they did not. It is unlikely that new houses were built between 1350 and 1450, and some fines which formerly included a messuage now only contained land. Probably the most telling evidence of bad times comes from the brevity of tenancies, names changed in one or two generations or less. No one gives up a good farm in good times.

The first sign of rejuvenation came after the middle of the 15th century.

Houses were rebuilt or repaired and, significantly, old virgates and half-virgates amalgamated to form the new landscape. If the old open field virgates of High Churt were no longer viable, two virgates or about sixty acres were possible (and so they stayed until the early 20th century). Although this revival started in a small way in the early Tudor period, the entry of the Luffs into Hide in 1503 marks the new era better. Not only did Churt change but also the documents that recorded it, henceforth more descriptive and copious. This was the period when High Churt was finally enclosed, and Piper, Foghell and Bat disappeared except as memories.

Notes

[1] One can, at least in imagination, hear an echo of a thousand years ago in the late Jim Voller's voice when he said to me of a long dead employer, "I took no mind of she, I just got on with me ploughing." He too once lived in the old house at Hide.

[2] A translation of *Frensham Beale Manor, 1342–7* (author's private papers) gives a good idea of what was grown on this poor soil.

[3] The late Jim Voller who supplied me with much valuable information and remembered Churt before the shops were built, once casually referred to Churt as "up there" meaning the area of High Churt. In the early 19th century Mayhew of 'Warryners' ('Old Barn') referred to the same thing when he objected to the siting of a church in Churt "as being too far from Churt".

[4] Map XVII opposite page 42

[5] see also page 38

[6] see also pages 39 & 54

[7] See Appendix

[8] Literally "none of the blood" which meant that a new tenant has taken on the land because no heir appeared at court to pay fine. Sometimes there was an heir but one could not or did not claim the land through poverty or some other reason.

Lanes, Farms and Places

Many of the old houses in Churt have been recorded by the DBRG and these are listed in the Appendix. Examples of fines in the Pipe Rolls and Fine Books relating to the various farms and places are given in the chapter on Manorial Fines. The schedule and map showing the location of various places and houses mentioned is on the next page; the numbers in square brackets refer.

The roads that meet at the The Pride of the Valley illustrate one of the many landscape changes which took place in the 1870s when the commons were enclosed by Act of Parliament. The resulting destruction of rural life was less in Churt than in many places. The farms no longer depended on the commons, though they continued to rob them for sand, stone, turf, and gorse. The most important change was to the roads. Many long-used roads across the commons were superseded by new straight ones; those to Thursley, Elstead and Tilford were made at that time. Jumps Road was also new, though it had been an old track. The level of the roads outside the Pride was also altered, the stream which formerly ran over it being channelled beneath (there is no record of a bridge). The old name of the road to Hindhead was Cresswell Lane. In the 16th century 'Cresswell' was the name given to the land to the east of the road. Here a spring feeds two ponds; ponds such as these were vital before the advent of piped water and some are very old. Most have now disappeared but can be found on the early OS maps.

The **Pride of the Valley** [1] is relatively new. The late Mrs Merrison had a large photo of the house at the end of the 19th century showing an auctioneer holding a small rural sale (from memory a cow and a calf, a pig, fowls, and oddments). Nothing could have so eloquently summed up the coming demise of farming in Churt, the auctioneer's chant a requiem for those Churt people who had toiled for centuries to turn this poor corner of west Surrey into something better than a Saxon 'Chart'. A few local surnames survive, unrecognised links with a distant past:– Voller, Bettesworth, Croucher, Clear, Norris, Matthew, and Larby; all have been common for 500 years, and one or two derive from the names of bondmen of 13th century Churt. West of the Pride of the Valley, along Jumps Road there is a house called **The Cedars** where there was formerly a public house called Devil's Jumps Inn. When Hindhead was opened up by the Victorians some old tracks across the commons became roads. The old public house was obviously superseded by the better-sited Pride.

Map showing key to Lanes, Farms and Places

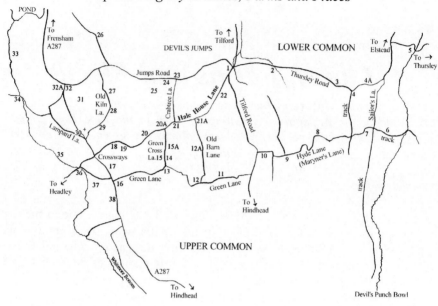

No	Place	Well	Pond
1	Pride of the Valley		
2	Stream Cottage		
3	Wolmer Cottage	√ behind house	
	Wey Cottage	√ behind cottage and house adjoining to west	
4	Hollands		
4A	Pitch Place		
5	Dye House		
6	Ridgeway Farm		√ in farmyard to west of house
7	Upper Ridgeway		√ on roadside opposite house
8	Hide	√ under room on west, 100ft deep, stone-lined	√ alongside entrance to farm building
9	Marchants Farm		
10	Stock Farm	√ ?behind house	√ on opposite side of road
11	Green Farm	√ on east of house	
12	Warreners	√ on east of house, 100ft+, covered, Tudor? brick-lined	

No	Place	Well	Pond
12A	Avalon		
13	Greencroft	√ under kitchen on north	
14	Greencross	√ north-east of house, 100ft+, covered	
15	Greencross Farm	√ south-west of former house	√
15A	The Toft		
16	Butts Farm	√ behind Hitchen Croft	
17	Quinettes	√ on opposite side of the road, slightly below cottage	
18	Hale House		√ by the roadside
19	Squirrels	√ east of house, close to wall	
20	Big Oak		
20A	Green Tye		√ on opposite side of road
21	Outmoor	√ south-east corner	
21A	Beyden's Hatch		
22	Varnolds		
23	Three Oaks		
24	Moorside		
25	White Croft		
26	Crosswater		
27	Old Kiln Lane		
28	Podmore	√ behind house	
29	The Old Forge		
30	Redhearn	√ behind house & √ on Green, almost opposite	√ on Green
31	Silverbeck		
32	Old Post Office		
32A	Beefolds	√ between road & site of demolished house	
33	Coppice Cottage		
34	Simmonstone		
35	Ivy Cottage		
36	Barford		
37	Kitts		
38	Hatch Farm		

Along the Thursley Road is **Stream Cottage** [2] (*see Fig 18*). The cottage which is late 17th or early 18th century, is something of a puzzle as it appears to occupy a site within ancient bondland but looks to be a typical medieval assart or perhaps more likely a Tudor encroachment. On the north side of the road there is a 19th century house named **Wolmer Cottage** [3] standing in a rectangular enclosure (*see Fig 19*). In contrast with the irregular boundaries of Well More a medieval assart to the east, the straight lines round this cottage show that it occupies an Enclosure Allotment. There are many references in the 17th century to a parcel of land called Wellmore containing 4 acres. The 'well' refers to the spring which rises there[1]. The eastern boundary of Hide was the eastern boundary of the tithing of Churt. Up to about 1940 it was a very large earthen bank now unfortunately obliterated as it may have dated from Caedwalla's grant of 688. **Pitch Cottage** on the south side of the road is a 17th century cottage now much altered, which was intact until about 1950.

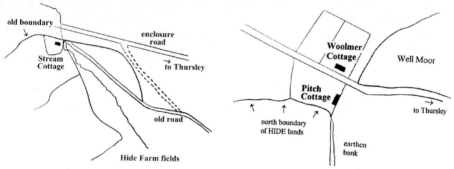

18: Stream Cottage   19: Wolmer Cottage and Boundaries

Further along the road at the corner of Maryner's Lane is a 19th century house called **Hollands** [4], a name which originated from hole land, or land at the bottom. The name Hollands is apparently an interesting example of folk memory. So far, this name has not been found in any document concerning Churt later than circa 1350 (and by that time it was already a memory being only repeated in the account under Defaults of Rent). Although its use elsewhere is common, indicating land at the bottom, it is a pleasant aberration for the OS map to locate it on high ground above Pitch Place: an example of how the meaning of names becomes confused over time. **Maryners Lane** is particularly interesting: not only for its name which is a reminder of the sailor who came to live there, probably on the east side, in the early 13th century, but also for the lane itself. It is the last of the old roads untouched by alterations except for the dreadful scouring by modern traffic and animals. The wide mouth where it joins the Green Lane shows what many road junctions were like before everything was enclosed[2]. The road junction is unusual for its two signs[3] which give the name and address of the person who lived there some 800 years ago: Maryner and Hollands.

70

Pitch Place [4A] is a difficult hamlet of which to write. The present parish boundary of Churt follows that of Hide Farm. It is claimed that it divided the tithing of Churt from that of Elstead. This looks dubious from the odd way in which it turns east along the Green Lane. Maryners Lane would be a more obvious boundary or even a continuation of Hide's boundary up the valley to the south. The problem should be solved by the early manorial fines, but not only do they fail to provide an answer, they make it virtually insoluble with some places being described randomly as in Churt and in Elstead. Pitch Place, for instance, well over the supposed boundary, was according to the manorial records always in Churt. To make matters worse Wey Cottage was held by Frensham Beale manor. It would not matter too much except that anyone reading later documents could be led wildly astray without knowledge of this awkward background. The house named Pitch Place is one of the larger houses in Churt. It came into the possession of the Paine family, one of whom (Thomas) was High Sheriff in 1717.

Wey Cottage replaced an earlier cottage called Lower Loompits. The earlier name derived from the loampit which formerly existed about half way up the west side of the road to the Ridgeways. It perhaps supplied the nearby pottery.

This tour along the lanes of Churt now enters into what was beyond doubt the tithing of Elstead. Nevertheless like Headley all this land up to the Punchbowl stream is inextricably bound up with Churt. Here again the long straight road is another enclosure improvement. The old one ran to the west, to Fullbrook. Crudescat, the rough place, was a strip of land on the west side of the stream above Truxford, taken out of the waste in the 12th or 13th century. It is difficult to imagine that the trickle of water under the road was once worthy of mention as a landmark on the Saxon boundary of the manor of Farnham.

To the north of the road to Elstead and Thursley is **Old Potters**, one of the small rural potteries that ceased working in the latter half of the 19th century It was probably similar to the one at Old Kiln. The straight road through Truxford is an enclosure road. The old road turned north down the steep hill beyond Old Potters and then along the valley to **Fullbrook**, a site long occupied. Fullbook is merely one variant of the numerous spellings.[4]

The Dye House [5] would not have been of particular note but for two things: its association with the Paine family and the survival virtually intact of an 18th century or earlier brewhouse. In the early 17th century the Paine family had the fulling mill at Pitfold. They seem to have prospered, coming to Churt later that century. In 1696 Paine bought the Hide lands from the Luffes, adding further properties in the following century. At that time one of the Paines studied law in London, and on returning to Farnham he set up (or joined) a business from which the present firm of Potter & Kempson is descended. By the end of the 18th century another of the Paines was in Frensham at the Rookery, farming the lands of Frensham Beale manor.

There would be nothing exceptional in this except for the fact that the surviving Paine documents provide valuable information on local matters. Of particular interest are those dealing with the dispute over the collection of tithes[5]. These papers are now preserved at the Farnham Museum and the Surrey History Centre. A few more are in private hands at Frensham.

To add more confusion to this corner of 'Churt', the narrow strip of Elstead land which runs up the Punchbowl was the Patifold, one of several '...folds' in south Surrey. Fines relating to Patifold include:

1283	12d	Seyld of Patifolde for her husband's land
1289	2/-	Adam of Patifolde for 2 acres purpresture from Cristina of Patifolde
1311		Robert son of Adam of Patifolde for 3 acres purpresture in Churt from Seylda of Patifolde, mother of Adam
1313	20/-	Robert of Patifolde for a messuage and ½ virgate surrendered by Robert of Holeland in Elstead
1317	10/-	Adam son of Robert of Patifolde for a messuage and ½ virgate from his father
1349	18d	Robert Childewell for a plot in Churt formerly held by Robert of Pattifolde

As the fines show, both Elstead and Churt had connections with the Patifold. Was it in Churt or in Elstead? In 1308 Patifold was described as being in Elstead and the land which 'the men of Elstead used to have'. In 1310 Stephen of the High Valley of Patifold (the Punchbowl) had half a virgate in Churt. This is less contradictory than may appear as Stephen's land was not necessarily in the Punchbowl. The Ridgeway fines of 1308 and 1310, one in Elstead the other in Churt, were again awkward but not impossible. The final blow to any argument comes from the Taxation of the 15ths and 10ths collected in 1332, in which each tithing is separately listed with the name of each person and the amount he paid. In the taxation list for Elstead tithing only two people can be identified with this area, both described as "of Crudescate". For the tithing of Churt the first three on the taxation list[6] are all of Patefield (sic), Adam, Nicholas, and Robert. The next are Robert and John of Ridgeway. Whether one believes the evidence of the fines or not seems irrelevant, as it is difficult to challenge the validity of the taxation lists for every tithing in the manor.

Ridgeways were ancient long-distance tracks which as far as possible avoided river valleys and woodland. In time the word came to be given to any upland path. One ran along the top of Firgrove Hill, south of Farnham. The two Ridgeway Farms in Churt suggest that the Green Lane following the contour from east to west was a ridgeway. Evidence from the Pipe Rolls suggests that the ridgeway was the old track running north-south through the Punchbowl to Hindhead and the coast. Local names bear witness to the fact that all the roads, lanes, and tracks to the south were used at one time or another by seafarers, smugglers, and others. The original 'maryner' of Churt was not, perhaps, a coincidence.

Ridgeway Farm [6]: The core of this house is what remains of an open hall for which a date from the early 15th century has been suggested by the DBRG. The fines reveal that an earlier house existed here in 1317. As much of this land went out of cultivation after about 1400, one would not expect a new house to have been built until late in the 15th century, say 1460–75. There may well be re-used timbers in it. This property can be traced in the manorial fines and documents under the name of Childewell or Zelds.

Upper Ridgeway [7]: This too was an open hall house. Its history can be traced by the name of Quedheps, a tenant of this farm in the 14th century.

Before the 16th century virtually all the documentary sources used and quoted for this study are of an impersonal nature. A few personal comments do creep into the Pipe Roll accounts, some being valuable. However, they are more the records of the observer than the participant. This changed dramatically after about 1500. Documents began to tell something of what the common people owned, did, and sometimes thought: Turner of the fulling mill at Standford tells his son (in his will) to work hard and look after his mother; John Huntingford pleads with his executors to look after his children; and William Bristowe's widow had a place by the fire at Hale House, reserved for her use.

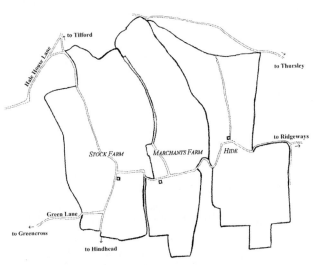

20: Stock, Marchants and Hide farms

The first purely family records are from **Hide** [8], the first being a copy of fine in the bishopric account giving title to Hide. Thereafter the records accumulated until Miss Wheeler[7] presented them to the Hampshire Record Office. The Luffs of Hide ceased holding land in Churt early in the 18th century An indirect link continued through the female line via the Chittys

73

and the Poultons to the Wheelers of Mill Court in Hampshire. The present house at Hide consists of two parts; the older part which is aligned with Green Lane was an open hall house. As there was a long gap in the list of fines after 1416 it is unlikely to have been built during that period, so it may be a survivor from the 14th century like Greencroft. In the core of the house, the blackened rafters could easily have been part of a simpler one re-used. The well at Hide uncovered in 1995 is over 100 ft deep to the surface of the water. It is stone lined, being of much better workmanship than the well at Greencross. The other part of the house, which has the most elaborate embellishment of any the Churt houses, was built in the early 17th century. Maps show a conventional farm plan with pond. Until the early 20th century there was a very large barn. The central road across the land was a public highway. Jim Voller recalled that the Council of the day objected to closure, but that a 'proper notice' was issued a day too late.

The earliest recorded tenant of **Marchants Farm** [9] was Robert Ryckman in 1320. The Ryckmans have the distinction of being the only[8] family in Churt that survived the Black Death as major landholders for any length of time, dying out as the fines show in 1593. There is unfortunately no particular medieval name for Marchants Farm. "Hide", "at Hide" and "of Hide" may have had significance at the time they were written but nothing can now be deduced.

Stock Farm [10] is of particular interest. Its land was built up from several medieval farms, including that of William Ryckman on the east side of the Tilford Road, and those of Carter and atte Stone on the west. The position of these lands in 1720 and in 1839 is shown in Fig 21.

Like Hatch Farm, the continuity of the fines bridges the gap between the medieval and modern Churt. Even the name "Stock" bears this out as it does not refer to livestock but to the stumps left when William Letice re-cleared atte Stone's land in 1451. These lands which make up Stock Farm may formerly have been demesne of the bishop. Split up into separate farms in the 13th century, they became amalgamated again for a short time in the 20th century. Through all those centuries none of its farmers achieved fame, or even notoriety, with the exception of the last, Lloyd George – and he wasn't a real farmer.

More than anywhere else in Churt, the land here evokes – to me at least – a sense of the continuity of the common people. Coming down the Tilford road there is for a hundred yards a view right across the Wey valley. The far crest beyond the castle is now dotted with houses. The generations who lived here would have seen it as Oteryngwode, slowly diminishing over the centuries.

Prior to the Black Death, **Green Farm** [11] had been two separate virgates. By 1359 the fine encompassed all the land between the Green Lane and the Hale House Lane, and was two virgates. In 1368 it was probably split up; what happened thereafter is uncertain until 1515 when the two virgates were again united. (At that date the Marchant's Farm and the Green

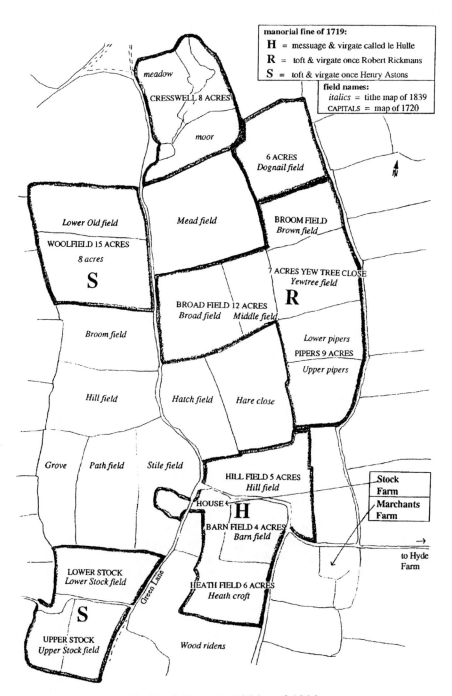

meadow

CRESSWELL 8 ACRES

moor

manorial fine of 1719:
H = messuage & virgate called le Hulle
R = toft & virgate once Robert Rickmans
S = toft & virgate once Henry Astons

field names:
italics = tithe map of 1839
CAPITALS = map of 1720

6 ACRES
Dognail field

N

Lower Old field

Mead field

BROOM FIELD
Brown field

WOOLFIELD 15 ACRES

8 acres

S

7 ACRES YEW TREE CLOSE
Yewtree field

R

BROAD FIELD 12 ACRES
Broad field   *Middle field*

Broom field

Lower pipers
PIPERS 9 ACRES
Upper pipers

Hill field

Hatch field   *Hare close*

Grove   *Path field*   *Stile field*

HILL FIELD 5 ACRES
Hill field

Stock
Farm

Marchants
Farm

HOUSE ←

H

BARN FIELD 4 ACRES
Barn field

→
to Hyde
Farm

LOWER STOCK
Lower Stock field

HEATH FIELD 6 ACRES
Heath croft

Green Lane

S

UPPER STOCK
Upper Stock field

Wood ridens

21: Stock Farm in 1720 and 1839

Farm fines are confusing since both had two virgates and both seem to have had land in Tilford. There was also a Greenrede near Truxford which adds to the confusion.) Early in the 17th century the two virgates were split again. The actual fields were identified of the virgate that went to the Shotter family. The Shotters were prominent local people, some of whom were officials who transacted bishopric business. The change of the name to "Greenhouse" in the 16th century shows how little is new and was perhaps as pretentious then as some of the new Churt names are today. Hale and Podmore also added "house" to their respective names. There was a further division of the land in 1611 when Thomas Boxall acquired a close called Widhanger of four acres on which was a cottage. The exact site is not known but it may possibly be where the house called **Woodhanger** stands today on the corner of Old Barn Lane. The field on the slope above Outmoor is named Widhanger; a name that seems to have been adopted for the whole of this small district.

Warreners [12]: The addition of "house" to the name of Green Farm is little more than a quirk when compared to what happened to the name of this farm. From about 1600 it was referred to as Warryners[9]. In many early accounts the name was written Warner, just as Marner was used for Maryner. This reflects the old pronunciation which pleasantly slurred the word, dropping the second syllable. This style of pronunciation was still heard occasionally twenty years ago. In the eighteenth century some scribe realised what had taken place and extended the name to Warreners[10]. On the first OS map the name was Mayhew's Farm, the name of the then occupant[11]. In the 1920s the name became Old Barn when the 17th century barn was converted to a dwelling house. It is uncertain when the name Warryners became attached to this land. The fines suggest that the Warner families had other properties before settling here. The purpresture land belonging to Warryners was to the south of Green Lane, on the opposite side of the road, 4 acres of which had been Hugh Lettice's in the late 14th century. A further 8 acres (probably two or more separate clearings but lying contiguously) went by the name of High Reeds, "reed" being the usual name given in the Farnham manor to land 'cleared out of the waste'. These asserts date from before the Black Death, and were acquired by Warner in the sixteenth century from Mant who held the virgates which make up Stock Farm.

The well here was reported to be lined with Tudor bricks. When it was discovered the then owner Mrs Howard was horrified to find it so inadequately covered. Twenty years ago when I identified the old house as "Warryners", Mrs Howard renamed it with its old name. Since then the old house, a pleasant open hall house with an internal jetty and a later crosswing, has changed its name to Old Barn Cottage, and its farm barn has become a manor house, Old Barn Manor.

Old Barn Lane which served Warryners was not connected to Green Lane until the 20th century, hitherto having ended in the farm yard. It was also used for access to Green Farm so as to avoid the steep hill between that farm and Warryners, branching off to the east above the copse opposite Avalon, turning south to Green Farm on the opposite site of the field.

At the bottom of Warryners' land where it met with the Outmoor boundary, fullers earth was found. How or when is not known, only that it was mined in the 16th and 17th centuries. There were two sites, one the land now occupied by **Avalon** [12A] and other the copse on the opposite site of the road. The two parts were named Pits Coppice and Pits Piece. Licences were granted as follows:–

1510	Richard Waryner – licence to dig fullers earth in Churt.
1538	Henry Upfold[12] – licence to dig fullers earth in Churt.
1567	William Upfold – licence to dig, for three lives.
1571	Robert Chandler – licence to dig, for three lives, below Richard Waryner's land.

With the increasing importance of the cloth trade in the Tudor period, many local mills were converted from corn to fulling. A new fulling mill was built in 1519 at Headley by Thomas Figg, just above the present mill pond. The fulling mill at Pitfold, long in decay, was also brought back into use in the following year.

The shape of the boundaries around the land enclosing **The Toft** [15A] is odd. The wavering eastern boundary indicates an early occupation, and therefore, in theory, it should be an assart, most of which can be clearly shown to jut out into waste or poor land from which it had been reclaimed. This one however does not, and more surprisingly it nudges into what is known to be bondland. Its origin must remain a subject of speculation. The house, originally a single bay cottage which was later extended by two bays towards the road, has seen a few name changes. During this century it has been known as Shiloh, Anne's Cottage, and The Toft, the latter name being selected by a recent occupier after reading the Wheeler Papers at the Farnham Library. In these papers Miss Wheeler suggested that this cottage was "the toft and one acre called Tarpeners", a supposition which has no support in the many documents concerning this Green Cross hamlet. The earliest reference to Tapeners (the correct spelling) in my papers comes from a default of rent in 1447 which reads as follows: "2 tofts; messuage and virgate and a toft and one acre called Tapeners and 18½ acres formerly of William Wayte etc no rent paid". As there was no punctuation, the entry can be read in several ways. In the defaults for Churt of that year, which was about the end of the depression following the Black Death, there were seven tofts and only one messuage. As a toft was a platform where a house once stood, it might be a reflection on the state of Churt housing at that time. Had I been Miss Wheeler I think I should have gone the whole hog and called the house "Tapeners".

Greencroft [13] and the adjoining enclosures of 3 acres and 6 acres of purpresture land (see Fig 22) are of special note for two reasons: firstly because the 3 acres gave the first clue to the antiquity of the hazel hedges and secondly for the house itself.

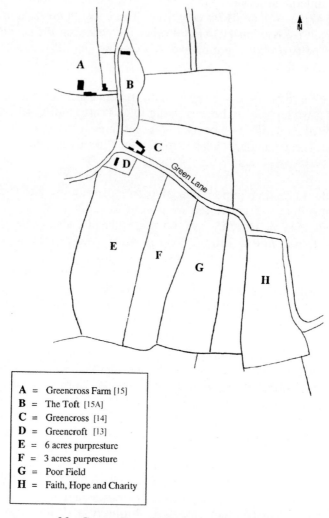

A = Greencross Farm [15]
B = The Toft [15A]
C = Greencross [14]
D = Greencroft [13]
E = 6 acres purpresture
F = 3 acres purpresture
G = Poor Field
H = Faith, Hope and Charity

22: Green Cross – houses and fields

When the house was recorded by DBRG it was seen to have passed through the usual stage of development from an open hall house, the presence of re-used timber being noted. When the present roof was remade, great flat blackened rafters were exposed. It is possible that they were original rafters from the old cottage, the present house being built around it. The fines show that there has been a cottage on the site since 1348 and by implication earlier. Although the DBRG has recorded many houses and accumulated a large reservoir of knowledge concerning their construction and development, it is rare to find documents which mirror their observations. It was difficult to believe that the hazel hedges which enclosed this croft were at least seven hundred years old, and that the messuage and the six acres adjacent on the west were those that Alice atte Wode surrendered to William atte Tounsend in 1348. The slight difference in acreage seen in the fines is not significant bearing in mind the difficulties in reading poor script and noting that the fines always revert to the three acres and six acres which it measures today. The three acres was probably on both sides of the stream which finally crossed Hale House Lane by Green Tye.

The lane between Waryners and Green Cross was apparently unused in the 19th century as the OS Map of 1870 marks it overgrown with bushes. On the south of the lane lay assarts of the 13th century and on the north the virgates described since the 14th century as "Tounsend" or "Tounsend or Wheeler". In the 17th century the name Green Cross was included in the fine description, "Tounsend or Wheeler" being dropped later. Green Cross is what remains of a typical west Surrey hamlet. The extent of the commons made any large farming area impossible resulting in a series of hamlets made up of three or four houses where virgates met at road junctions, in this case, Greencroft, Greencross, The Toft, and the house of Greencross Farm (now demolished). The Tounsend virgate was on the east side of Greencross Lane.

Greencross [14]: This house was of three bays with a central smokebay. The well on the east side of Greencross, discovered during alterations to the house, was found to be over 100 ft deep and stone-lined.

What is now called **Greencross Farm** [15] is one of the last working farms in Churt. Although now more extensive, it is thought to have included a part of Hidland, the purpresture land cleared by the de Hide families in the 13th century. A connection with the Luffe family certainly dates from 1539 when Thomas Philpe leased his messuage and two virgates to William Luffe. From 1586, when Ann née Philpe the wife of John Luffe inherited the land, until the late 19th century it was held from the bishopric under a copyhold tenancy by the Luffe family and their descendants; the last by that name, John Luffe, died in 1705. When the farm was sold in 1854, the sale particulars stated that two heriots, an ox in each case, were payable but that £5 was generally accepted in lieu of each heriot.

The old house, the site of which is behind the present bungalow, was demolished early in the 20th century. The farm buildings still in use consist of a 16th century barn and a small range of brick buildings circa 1800. The large size of the barn is interesting as it supports the idea that local barns – every farm had one – were built for general storage rather than solely for corn. In fact, not much corn was ever grown in Churt and Headley prior to the late 18th century except perhaps on a few of the larger farms like Wishanger. In the centre of the farm yard there was a pond, apparently fed by a spring. The water from it flowed freely down Greencross Lane until about 1960 when it was piped underground. The spring dried up soon after that.

Butts Farm [16] Until the name of Browns Farm was found on Bryant's Map of 1823 there was considerable uncertainty whether the name "Browns" in various fines referred to a farm of the same name in Frensham. Once the authenticity of "Browns" in Churt was established it then became possible to follow the fines. The Brown fines and their ramifications are more complicated than any others in Churt. They showed that, contrary to all previous evidence, Greencross Lane was not the end of the westward extension of bondland. Furthermore the Butts-Brown lands ran west-east, from the A287 along the north side of Green Lane to Greencroft, and did not conform to the other lands which ran north-south. This made study of west Churt even more complicated. The name Browns Farm changed to Butts Farm in the 19th century though no person of that name has been found. After Aldershot was established as a military establishment possible shooting ranges were surveyed in the adjacent countryside. An OS map in my possession shows several ranges in Churt, and one pencil line which runs between Butts and one of the Jumps suggests the probable origin of the name. Butt's house, much altered, contains old timbers. Its barn dates from about 1600 or a little earlier.

The Brown fines can be traced back to William le Fre in 1306. The family name of Fre is not found anywhere else in the manor of Farnham, nor in Headley, nor is its pronunciation certain. Many of the names included in the fines are written with variations of spelling which assist in ideas on pronunciation – one later version of the name is given as "Fray". Although "free" is an obvious interpretation, one would have expected an earlier extended version viz: the freeman[13] but that name does not occur. If one looks at other fines associated with the Fre family, all the traceable lands were to the west of Churt. These fines throw an unexpected light on land settlement in west Churt, showing that part of it was bondland and already occupied by consolidated holdings in the early 1200s or earlier.

Green Lane and the A287 (*see Fig 23*). In some ways the road at Butts Farm epitomises the change from old rural Churt to what it was to become. The old highway which had served Churt for centuries was degraded to a lane whilst the rough track across the common to Hindhead was elevated to a highway. This was the birth of the A287 and with it Churt had finally been severed from its Saxon past. The latest phase is now going ahead as old wandering paths are being converted to roads suitable for all manner of wheeled vehicles. Some social divisions have gone – where formerly there were three classes of exhibitors at the flower show, now there is only one, and gone too are the dreadful housing conditions of the early 20th century. Churt is no longer a farming area. It never was a village, nor is it today, not even a dormitory conglomeration. But this is to digress, as the road did. At the start of the century the A287 beyond Hatch Farm was little more than a sheep track across the common. An advertisement of the time stated that there was a man at Hindhead who had a conveyance and would take visitors to Frensham Pond – as he knew the way!

The course of the A287 was straightened with the advent of motor buses. The old road from the south turned east as far as Butts and then down the deep cutting to the **Crossways**. The old inn, a typical three or four bay 16th century house, features in many local publications. The framing on the south west, the weather side, has gone being replaced with rubble and Bargate. At one time it was called The Shant, a word that cannot be found in the OED. With the addition of a "y", it may be a description of what the inn became. No doubt it had served its time, but its successor from the outside at least does little credit to the brewery which commissioned it.

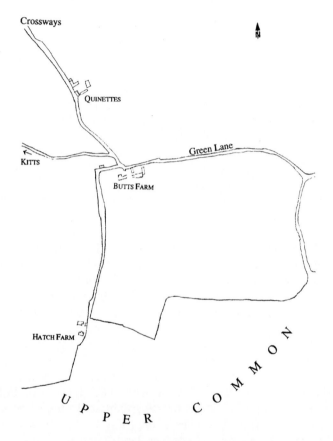

23: Roads at Butts farm in 1839

Quinnettes [17]: This house is thought to have been a conventional smoke bay house, though it was so thoroughly altered circa 1920 together with old farm buildings adjacent, that it is difficult to be more precise. It is curious that its barn, one of the largest in Churt, was built to store the produce of one of the worst pieces of land. The name Quinnettes first appears in a document of 1575, when Henry Pyninge bought it together with

2 yardlands. The same document also contained the sale of Hale to Richard Brystowe and of Pipers to William Brystowe respectively, both of whom were described as shearmen[14]. All these lands were said to be in the manor of Hale. Two hundred years later, the Quinnettes' land, renamed Parkhurst, consisted of a narrow strip of land between Hale House Lane and Jumps Road. Quinnettes, other than as a personal name, has no meaning in itself but it may be derived from a similar name "quillette"[15], which when associated with land refers to a narrow strip.

From the Crossways, formerly with a wooden signpost in the middle of the road and a gate into an open field opposite the inn, the road turns east. Now named **Hale House Lane**, it was formerly called Shant Lane. Jim Voller, who passed on to me invaluable memories of old Churt, knew it as the Nether Lane, probably a much older and more accurate name. The road between the Crossways and Crabtree Lane, though now little more than a racetrack for commuters, is worth more than a cursory glance for it is in itself another small part of the story of Churt (*see Fig 4*). The car driver might say that it is narrow and tortuous, but little more. He would hardly use the word 'switchback' and yet that would once have been more appropriate. This is not difficult to illustrate:– from the Crossways the road rose gently to about level with the end of the Playing Field, with Hale House at the top of a sharp rise; it then followed a steep drop to the stream which ran through The Meadows and across the road to Old Kiln, another sharp rise and a level stretch brought it to Big Oak, it then descended to the stream, rising and falling again to the junction with Greencross Lane. It is only when looking carefully at the contours adjacent to the road that the extent of the switchback becomes clear. This was certainly no road for wheeled traffic, nor was it needed as such. Even in the 16th century few of the local farmers had carts. This was an old track. It is easy to imagine it developing over the centuries with the passage of animals, wild and domestic, and men who wandered here. In fields on both sides of the lane, prehistoric worked flints of all ages are common.

Hale House [18] and more particularly its land is a puzzle before the document of 1572 (*see Quinnettes*) when the property was purchased by Richard Bristowe. The land which went with Hale House[16], on both sides of the valley towards Old Kiln, was almost certainly a 13th century clearing of the waste. By 1624 various branches of the Bristowe family also had Browns (Butts Farm) and Greencross as well as land adjacent to the Furlong and Greencroft, all of which were connected both by location and fines. Prior to 1634, Pudmore was a part of Hale House land. In 1661 Hale House and its land passed from the Bristowe family via a daughter Rebecca and her husband Richard Smart to Richard Lutman for £300. Thereafter it became the property of The Queen's College, Oxford. The house incorporates remnants of an old open hall built possibly in the early 16th century with a later crosswing added by the Bristowe family. In William Bristowe's will of 1634, a clause stated that his widow Elinor was to have use of the lower room called "the cupperd chamber standing westward" and £10 per year[17]. The well at Hale House is said to contain a rifle thrown down by a soldier returning from the 1914–18 war. The barn dates from about 1600.

The early history of **Squirrels** [19] is unknown. For the last two hundred years or more it seems to have been a tenanted property, attached either to Hale House or to Greencross Farm which adjoins it on the other side. The name is of uncertain origin. There is another house of the same name at Kennel Farm in Frensham and both are small properties adjoining more substantial ones. The present house is formed from the remaining half of the original house. Like many in Churt, particularly in the 18th–19th century, it became divided into two tenements. (Some were occupied by three families in the 19th and early 20th centuries.) The bishopric estates presentations 1749 confirm this division: "We present Henry Craster for not keeping in tenantable repair two tenements, one in the possession of the said Henry and the other in occupation of John Gamblin which if not speedily repaired will be detrimental to the lord of the said manor and also of the said John Gamblin whose right it will be on the death of Sussanna the present wife of the above Henry Craster." This is another long-occupied site; it is a pity that it cannot be identified from the early fines.

At **Big Oak** [20] is one of the few trees to escape regular cropping and replacement with spontaneous new growth and is, according to Alan Mitchell's tables, about 300–350 years old. If nothing is done to change the present policy, the treescape of Churt will have entirely changed in the next 50–100 years, as it already has on the east where few trees now remain. Few young oaks grow and none have their side branches trimmed up to a fair height before being allowed to spread. Nearly opposite Big Oak the roadside hedge contains a short length of double hazel (*see Fig 6*). Lower down it peters out where sheltering cattle have eroded the inner row. The junction with Greencross Lane is one of the few places whose successive levels of erosion are clearly visible. The position of the stone[18] on its eastern side shows that it once had a curve which matched the old higher level below the garden of Minnfordd, similar to the south end of Maryners Lane. Old maps show other similar junctions that have since been squared up. Greencross Lane has the remains of a double hedge as far as the farm road on the east. Thereafter the east hedge and track is relatively new compared with the eroded hazel one on the other side.

A hundred yards further along Hale House Lane another stream once crossed the road. Until this century there was a large pond on the south side of the road. Until enclosed in 1870s **Green Tye** [20A] was a small common; Bryant's map named it Cowleg. Opposite Green Tye on the south there is a farm gate which allows the huge erosion bank on the far corner of the field to be seen. In some 800 years a sloping field has become nearly level. It is this kind of erosion which has made the switchback effect of the Lane described above much less evident than formerly.

Outmoor [21] The earliest part of the present house was built in the 16th century with a smoke bay. It occupies a site of considerable antiquity; the earliest fine dates from 1228. The field which rises to the crest of the hill on the south of Outmoor is now called Woodhanger. In earlier documents it was always Widhanger, causing confusion with Wishanger. The small hanger is at the crest on the west side of the field. At the foot of the hill there is a depression where fullers earth was dug in the 18th century.

The land round about the junction with Old Barn Lane became muddled over the centuries. In 1257 John de Hale, David de Hale, Robert de Clere and Walter Alleyn cleared 13½ acres of land, part of which, possibly all, was on the north side of the road. For the next 750 years, four properties came to have plots of land attached to their virgates described as "in the common furlong". The Furlong was a part of this land and the name "Alleyn" with field names were added to its deeds in about 1900.

In 1332 one acre of waste here was granted to Richard Beyden. He disappeared with the Black Death, and of his rent of 3d nothing was paid in 1348. Hereabouts was one of the gates that separated the farm lands from their commons, referred to centuries later as **Beydenshatch** [21A]. It is uncertain whether it was on Hale House Lane or at the bottom of Old Barn Lane. Early in the 20th century there was a gate about 50 yards up Old Barn Lane.

Varnolds [22] is on an ancient site. The OS map of 1870 showed it as having a complete set of farm buildings, all of which have now disappeared. Until the early 20th century it had a timber-framed barn. It has not been possible to identify this land with certainty through the fines, but it may have been the land which the Carter and Cuper families held in the 13th century. Part of the modern farm extended along Hale House Lane, the rest along the Tilford Road, and only the latter would have been within the boundary of High Churt. *It has been possible to see the deeds of Varnolds since this was written. The name entered into them was Fernhill which is a clue to the name Varnolds.[19] It shows the old drawled pronunciation of ER as AR, as in Ferneham and Farnham.*

On the opposite side of the road there is a series of fish ponds. The upper one was made in the early 17th century by one of the Luffes, from whom the bishop required a yearly rent for the "floodgates below Fernhill". Nearby, on the east side of the road, W Rankine, one-time schoolmaster at Churt and an elected member of the Royal Society, excavated a very considerable Mesolithic site.

Jumps Road passes through what was formerly waste or common land until the Enclosures of the 1870s. This area of Churt is interesting for illustrating the existence of the old 'ways'[20]. These were the tracks which had come into existence because they were the best cross-country paths for passage and distance, and they are almost certainly of considerable antiquity. Many of these ways shown on the tithe map have now disappeared, others are still footpaths although their routes have often been altered by landowners. Jumps Road is a example of a "way". Even in the 1950s it was not much of a road by modern standards, nor would it be now if it had not been improved so as to take traffic away from Hale House Lane (in which it has not succeeded).

On the corner of Jumps Road is **Three Oaks** [23] Many years ago, Bill Croucher told me that before the 1914–18 war the then occupier used to grow potatoes on Outmoor Green, now called Green Tye. He also said that Three Oaks contained some thick walls, which implied that it was built round the remains of an earlier house, from which it was claimed to have some rights on the common. Documents and maps reveal a rather different story. The 1839 tithe map showed no house on the site of Three Oaks though there was a cottage and garden by the roadside adjoining the eastern hedge of Moorside. By 1870 a new house, Three Oaks had replaced the cottage[21] on a new site. On the opposite side of Crabtree Lane there still remain the footings of another small building. It is uncertain whether this was an illegal squat on the waste or whether it was a farm building attached and built with Three Oaks. At the time of the enfranchisement of the copyhold in 1895, Three Oaks was held by "Louisa Edith Karn[22], late of John Newman, (securing the right of Mary Ann Newman and Edward Newman, deceased)". It consisted of "a cottage or tenement and shop with garden, turf house, fuel house and a small piece of arable land adjoining called Copse Field". Moorside and Warreners Mead were also included in the Karn property.

The name **Warreners Mead** indicates that this meadow with the house probably belonged to the farm of that name on the Green Lane, and it certainly did. Until root crops were grown in the 17th–18th centuries, over-wintering of livestock was difficult, as already described. Nevertheless some animals had to be kept for essential work the following spring and for this purpose hay was vital. On the light land of Churt crops of natural grass were relatively poor and in dry or wet years could be negligible. As a result those pieces of valley land naturally wet or capable of being flooded or irrigated were of great value: in cash terms four times that of the best wheat land. When possible, land even at a distance was acquired for its hay value, eg Ridgeway in Churt had an acre in Elstead. Warreners Mead was Warrener's hay field. Although most traces are now obliterated, there were formerly tiny pieces of hay meadow all along the stream by the Jumps Road, some are now lawns. The value of a hay meadow can be appreciated from the following passage in the Headley Survey of 1552, which recorded that:– "Roger Yalden did hold one acre of meadow called Thurstone mead and the first crop[23] of one acre of meadow with John Heath in Kings mead and the first crop in two butts with …". Bill Croucher told me that a local man, name now forgotten, had achieved the feat of mowing with a scythe the whole of Warreners Mead in one day.

Moorside [24] is of special interest being one of the few really old cottages whose date of building is known. Both ends have been extended or altered and the roof is a later replacement. Mortices for dragon ties can be seen in the wallplate. The Pipe Roll account of 1341 recorded a grant of 3 rods 7 perches of waste in Churt to Osbert le turner. The rent was to be 3d per annum. Osbert's widow inherited the property in 1346 and by then a cottage had been built. She presumably died in the Black Death as rent was in default in 1348. The record is not clear but it was probably empty for some years before becoming attached to Warryners. It might be questioned why such an insignificant cottage survived so long. The answer lies in the question: because it was small and occupied only a small plot. Houses on the old virgates were, almost without exception, modified or demolished and new ones built in their place. The cottage did not justify such expense as there was insufficient land to support anything larger. Moorside once had outbuildings similar to those of Three Oaks: the outside oven has now gone, having given way to sliced bread, and electricity has taken the place of the fuel or turf house. In the early part of the 20th century Moorside was split into three tenements.

There were two distinct periods when there was social pressure to extend land occupation into the commons, the first of which the pre-1348 assarts have already been described. The second period was a persistent invasion of the commons in the 17th and 18th centuries also caused by an increasing population. Settlement was resisted as far as possible but some encroachment did take place. It was sometimes possible to build a house, probably little more than a shed, then if not dispossessed a better one would be erected later. In normal cases the tithingman would present the matter to the manor court and the occupier would be told to pull it down within a certain time. It was rarely done. If the family proved to be of good account over a number of years, a petition backed by substantial tenants of the manor might ask the bishop to grant a copy: that is to regularise the position and grant a normal copyhold tenure. An example of such an encroachment may be **White Croft** [25] which is a small cottage, built in the late 18th or early 19th century, that could well have replaced an earlier small building. There is an undated petition[24], which may even have been for White Croft, signed by John Luffe the elder, Henry Ockley and Richard Mathew. It is a good example of how it was done. Henry Ockley died in 1710, so the petition was made prior to that date. Alternatively 1762 when a large number of new copyholds were granted is another possible date for this house. It is perhaps significant in this context that White Croft was declared to be tithe-free when sold in 1854. It then consisted of house, barn, stable, shed, and piggeries together with 9 acres divided into three fields. The garden east of the stream was coppice, west of it was meadow. The land now occupied by Brook House was arable. The stream was then stated to be feeding a trout pond. It was let to James Wheeler for £9 per annum and sold for £325.

The footpath which now runs past White Croft to Old Kiln formerly ran in a straight line from Three Oaks, coming out near the pond. Many other old paths have been similarly altered to suit the convenience of landowners. The ordinary people who used them were unable to resist pressure from those who might employ them or their dependants.

There is nothing in the medieval history of Churt that can be specifically linked with **Crosswater** [26]. In looking at Churt, or even at the ancient documents, it is easy to forget that it was more like an island in the waste than a nice tidy park-like area. There were still, and probably remained so until the late 15th century, pockets of relatively untouched woodland. The many references to them via the two woodwards and the Perquisites of the Court confirm this. With this background it seems improbable that Crosswater was settled at that time to the extent that it came to be in the early 20th century. What it was, or what it certainly became, was a valuable area of water meadows. When irrigation started is unknown; it is a simple and obvious method of growing hay, and evidence of it exists in early accounts. One would have expected it to have been linked to the larger Churt farms, as were Warreners Mead, Whitmore Vale, and the Hale Meads on Frensham Common.

The changing of names makes description difficult so the houses will be described starting from Jumps Road. The first one on the left, now renamed **Crosswater Mill** (no mill ever existed here) was constructed from a shed shown on the tithe map. The barn is probably late 17th century and is referred to in Thomas Newman's will of 1726 (*see below*).

The next house on the left, The Barn now re-named **Crosswater Barn**, is more interesting. The front, probably circa 1700, is comparable to Old Kiln. The original timber-framed house was on the north side of the present one, at right angles to the road. Part of the framing on the west side was intact in the mid 1970s. Some of the timbers from the original house are probably those re-used inside the house when the wall of the living room was altered. The description of the house in Thomas Newman's will[25] shows that it was of modest proportions, as would be expected when little land was attached to it, and the surviving timbers[26] are much smaller than those used in most Churt houses. At the start of the 20th century it was held of the manor by John Larkby[27], letter carrier. His daughter, Mrs Fowler, lived in the house until her death in about 1976. At that time all the old fireplace fittings, cranes, etc were still in place, just as they had been when she was a girl, although of course not in use. Mrs Fowler, like Bill Croucher, supplied valuable information about the old Churt. Two pieces have stayed in mind. First, they used to bake their bread every three weeks. In the intervening weeks it was kept in the cold oven, not a bad place since it was rendered sterile at regular intervals. The second, undoubtedly more surprising at the time, concerned her father's (or grandfather's) gun. This was a muzzle-loader kept just below the ceiling over the open fire. Contrary to modern practice it was always kept loaded. This was not known to a young visiting relative. He, seeing it cocked, took it down to release the hammer. Bungling this, the gun fired. Luckily the ball missed the people in the room which was filled with smoke from the powder. What made the fireplace unique, not only in Churt but in other houses recorded by DBRG in Surrey, was the small powder cupboard fixed at the side of the beam over the hearth. The obvious place to keep the powder dry, it still contained flask, powder, ball, and wadding. I was sorry then, and have been so ever since, that the whole hearth and fittings could not have been preserved complete.

The penultimate house and farm buildings on the right side of the road, referred to in documents as **Crosswater Farm**, are good examples of the new farm buildings of the 18th or early 19th centuries. No specific documentation has been found relating to them. By that date small estates had come into being and individual documents often become lost amongst estate papers.

The last house on the same side of the road has the distinction of once having been the workhouse.

The old meadows were broken up in the 19th century when the first modern houses were built. With plenty of cheap labour, fish ponds and ornamental ponds were made by damming streams and diverting the old irrigation channels. Mrs Fowler told me that before the war they always flooded their little meadow. Afterwards they were unable to do so because their water had been diverted. I flooded the adjacent meadow for the last time in the 1950s.

Old Kiln Lane leaves Jumps Road with what was called Podmores on the west side and Dutton's Hill Common on the east. The ponds on the Silverbeck side are modern and until 1950 they were bordered by gardens with bulbs and primulas. **Old Kiln** [27] now much altered contains the old thick Bargate walls and is an early example of this type of Churt house. Recently further information has come to light concerning the two acre plot of land on which Podmore and Old Kiln stand. This plot was one of the 13th century assarts made by the occupiers of Hale. The remains of the bank which enclosed it from the common still exist above the present gardens. More immediately informative are the photocopies of wills and inventories produced by Mr Jason S Pope, a descendant of the Moses Mullard who built the Old Kiln house and the pottery. These show that Moses, a potter from Aldershot born in 1674, acquired the two acres in the last decade of the 17th century. His first three children were born in Aldershot, Moses the eldest in 1699. His fourth child was christened in Frensham in 1704. It seems probable that he lived in the old house at Podmore whilst building a new house and pottery. The descriptions of the property in the first Moses will is interesting; the will is dated 1728 and he died the following year. The "Old Tenement called Podmore" was still standing. With it was included "The pott Kiln, Barn, Shopp, Warehouse, Garden and Outhouses". To his wife he left his "New Tenement with ground below the path and fewell house thereunto belonging". To his son George he left "the meadow ground and coppice ground by estimation 2 acres called Pudmore". The second Moses had no surviving son and the property descended to the eldest of his three daughters, Ann who married a Dutton thus beginning the connection of this land with the Duttons which lasted into the early 20th century.

The bishopric estates papers at the HRO contain numerous presentments against the Mullards for using turf for firing the pottery "for burning turf or soyl of the lord in his pott house for burning Earthen Ware (sic) for sale over and above what he uses in necessary uses for family use. He shall be amerced 20/- per load in future". There also seem to have been disputes as to whether Ann was the true heir. The pottery was carried on until the late 19th century (the date is uncertain). I remember Jim Voller telling me that they used to cart clay from the dell which was east of Greencroft. The kiln was intact until about 1950, the dome collapsing the following year. Permission to excavate was granted in 1976 when the property was being sold. The work was expertly carried out and the site neatly cleaned up. It revealed three layers of flue one above the other. The two excavators made no report and failed to provide the then owners with promised photographs. Their names were lost and it has not been possible to trace them. Locally the Old Kiln dip became known as Dutton's Hollow. Little of the old pottery remains in Churt, though numerous fragments turn up of which there should be samples in the Farnham Museum.

Podmore [28] The name Pud- or Podmore is not uncommon and is usually associated with puddle – mud. To me as a farmer with my experience of the slope behind it, the suggestion of boggy land is not inappropriate, the more so if one reflects on what it was probably like centuries ago with a higher water table. This land is an early clearing of the Hale valley. The name Pudmore, dignified by the addition of "house", first appeared in a document of 1634 relating to Hale House viz: "... Hale House and three score acres, excepting pudmore house and the land belonging which is twelve/twenty acres more or less" (twelve in one document and twenty in another). This original attachment to Hale explains why at a much later date Podmore had land near or opposite Outmoor, this land having formerly been part of the Hale lands along Hale House Lane. By the 1830s the house (*see comments on Old Kiln above*) had disappeared, there being none on the tithe map. The present house with a small range of farm buildings dates from circa 1850. Early in the 20th century the front room on the north side was a little shop. There used to be one of the most magnificent wisterias in Churt climbing over the barn, part of which also served as a bakehouse.

There is no evidence that the present green was ever more than part of the common before the church was built. Documents have revealed the existence of two early house sites and their lands, **The Old Forge** [29], and **Redhearne** [30] or Pipers. The tithe map shows fields behind Old Forge, now part of the playing field, as named Philips, and a small copse at the end of Old Kiln Close called Filpe's Rough. A document in the Minet Library, Borough of Lambeth, dated 17th April 1793 describes this land:– "A messuage or dwellinghouse called by the name of Philps and also land on which it stands, and also one barn erected there, also garden etc and five closes of land (11 acres) adjoining the messuage". This is of particular value as it adds to accumulating evidence that Churt, certainly west Churt, was composed of a great number of very small fields before about 1800. As with Hale House and Quinnettes, no manorial fines can be traced to the land with certainty, nor to Woodyers or Redhearne alias Pipers, and so this small part of the Churt story must remain something of a blank.

A string of references can be associated with **Silverbeck** [31]. The name of "Hooks" is first linked with this property in a manorial fine paid in 1458 by Robert Derby. In John Padyk's fine of 1508 both Hooks and Brown were coupled together under the same ownership, as well as a virgate once of Roger Free and an unnamed half virgate. As there were three parcels of land in Churt all called Hooks and all of about the same acreage there is some confusion over their later history; added to which the artist who acquired Silverbeck in the mid-19th century was also named Hook! The tithe map shows two fields just to the south of the house called Upper and Lower Hooks. Also called Hooks was the hook or hook-shaped piece of land on the east side of the Barford Stream where it enters Frensham Pond. It was probably cleared with the adjacent Hale land in the early 14th century when it was described as Hokesrede: the hook-shaped clearing. This name continued on records down to the 16th century with variable acreages and spellings; on many occasions Hokes. The old house at Silverbeck has been gutted, possibly by the artist Hook for a studio. It possesses one of the few remaining wells with a well top, and a much-altered 16th century barn with later buildings which were still in use in the early part of the 20th century. The remains of the pottery kiln which apparently continued after the Old Kiln closed down are about 20 yards in from Jumps Road.

Such a maze of fines and documents surrounds the lands in west Churt that it is irritating to be unable to disentangle their medieval origins. One might reflect that what is written down here in a couple of hours and read in 15 minutes took place over three centuries, and that Murphy's Law applied just as much to the people of those generations as it does to mechanical devices today. The most accomplished scribe was just as likely to make a mistake as the most efficient modern press.[28]

At the junction of Jumps Road and the A287 was another of the tiny hamlets as previously described under Green Cross. At the end of Jumps Road is the **Old Post Office** [32] where in the early 20th century you could buy both loose sugar and gunpowder! The house still retains its original frame on the north; this side always survives better, being somewhat protected from wind and rain. Although the house has been there since the 16th century, no documentary evidence has been found through which it can be positively identified. Being on the edge of the common it is likely to have had a small plot deriving from an early assart of the 13th or early 14th century. This idea is somewhat supported by land opposite, formerly **Beefolds** [32A], which was certainly an assart of the 13th or early 14th century. It was described in the Consistory Court Rolls of 1714 as: "2 fields of 6 acres called Beefolds on the road from Barford to Farnham" when it was transferred or sold by John Denyer to Alexander Mose. An old house on this land, shown by the OS Map of 1870 to have been on the roadside, was demolished by Abbot who bought both this property and the adjacent one in the late 19th century. Some of the old farm buildings still exist. The name

Beefolds was later transferred to his new house on the road to Farnham. The old house that Abbott demolished was probably the Star Inn. The hill leading up to Barford and Simmonstone is still sometimes remembered as Star Hill.

The boundary between Frensham and Churt is still marked in one place by the remains of an old bank. It is situated a few yards north of the bus stop at the south east corner of Frensham Pond. Growing on it are a few straggling branches of a thorn bush. At the start of the 20th century when the commons were largely bare of gorse and bracken this thorn was a solitary and rather imposing bush, so much so that 'meet me at the thorn' needed no further qualification. One wonders what it might have once signified as such solitary thorn boundary marks are not uncommon elsewhere.

The narrow strip of cultivatable land alongside the Barford Stream between Frensham Pond and the south end of Whitmore Vale has a history which differs greatly from that of High Churt. This is possibly due to a much later initial occupation, although there is always the possibility that the clearing of the waste here in the early 13th century was no more than a re-clearing. The northernmost part, between Frensham Pond and **Coppice Cottage** [33], was land of the de Hale family. The cottage is probably on the site of the first assart of the early 13th century. The fines show that further plots were cleared bit by bit, culminating in the last six acres next to Frensham Pond in 1343 (*see Fig 3*). The banks with which the de Hales enclosed their lands, though now much eroded, still give a idea of what they were like when new. They are far worthier of careful preservation than some heritage features on which money is expended. Coppice Cottage, now modernised, still retains features which suggest a date circa 1600. The great stones from the old floors now serve as garden paths. The hollow track on the south side of the cottage was formerly a public road to Field House and Wishanger. Now blocked, it is reduced to a footpath. Jim Voller remembered using it for horse and cart. This cottage is of special interest as it was here that Bill Croucher lived as a boy. The story that he wrote[29] of it many years later is one of the best that has been written since Sturt and his Bettesworth sagas. Unlike Sturt, it is the chronicle of a participant rather than an observer. Behind the cottage there was a series of small irrigated meadows, mostly on the Headley side of the stream.

Simmonstone or Symondstone [34], although in Headley, is sufficiently near to Churt to need at least a note. The present name derives from a Seman who formerly held the sub-manor of Wishanger. The stone which marked the boundary was still in place by the stream until about 1945–50; then, like all the other ancient boundary stones, it was removed, whether by the Council or purloined for a rockery is unknown.

The road between Lampard House and Barford was formerly the main road between Pitfold (Shottermill), Grayshott, Frensham, and Farnham. In several places erosion of the banks on both sides of the lane suggests that there had once been dwellings on the east side, of which only **Ivy Cottage**[30] [35] remains today. The present house replaces an earlier timber framed one.

The site is ancient and was still known by the old name of Woodyers when the OS map of 1870 was surveyed. The first definite reference is in a document amongst the Wheeler Papers dated 4 November 1572. It describes the sale by William Gregory of Shalden, Hants for £29 of "messuage with buildings and gardens called Woodyers with one yardland". A later document of 1641 describes Woodyers as having a house, barn and six closes of land, 15½ acres. This description together with that for the land of The Old Forge gives a better picture of old Churt than all the other documents put together. If one looks over the gate by Ivy Cottage towards Barford Court, it is difficult to imagine that this land was once tiny fields, a landscape exactly as described for Headley in the survey of 1552[31].

The **Barford** [36] or Bereforde in early accounts, has been a landmark of consequence for many centuries. First recorded in a charter of AD 909, it marked the boundary between what became the counties of Surrey and Hampshire. In early records it included the land between a trackway (the present A287) and the stream and roughly from Simmonstone to Whitmore Vale. Now the name of Barford is used more narrowly. Above Barford the old road splits into two, one running up each side of the valley. It seems curious that the remaining houses and traces of demolished ones are on the western side rather than on the eastern side closer to Churt. The reason for this becomes clearer if one reads the 1552 survey of Headley. The road down the west side of Whitmore Vale was described as a "highway", continuing as it does straight across the Headley Road. The track on the east side of the valley was a "way", the name used for any casual path, and it only provided access to the mill. The houses were therefore built along the highway.

Nearby are several small quarries. It was from these that karrs (carrstones) were taken to repair the dams of the two Frensham ponds in 1396 and 1406. In those accounts the names of local men and how much they earned were given in full: John Collin of Greencroft did eight days' work in 1396 and was paid 8d per day.

Above Barford there are the remains of three mills, all now converted into houses. The lower one next to the Headley road bridge, and the upper one below the large mill pond are relatively modern. These mills were constructed for industrial purposes such as paper and flock milling. The middle mill, always a corn mill, has occupied the present site since 1343; prior to that date it had been on the Churt side of the river. In that year the Churt mill was transferred to the Headley side of the stream; no reason was given for this move. One can only guess that the old mill was in disrepair and the opportunity was taken to move to a better site (by that time Headley had become part of the bishopric of Winchester). This mill is one of the only two mills[32] in the manor of Farnham which continued to mill corn throughout the centuries. All the others appear to have changed to, or incorporated, a fulling mill at one time or another.

The Barford lands seem to have been cleared haphazardly. Above the Headley road, between the A287 and the stream, the record of clearing can be ascertained from the fines. There may have been an ancient colony of smiths here from an early date; clearances by them appeared in accounts from about mid-13th century. By 1291 the 23 acres of purpresture (which featured in every fine for the land of **Hatch Farm** [38] for the next six and a half centuries) was inherited by Mary, widow of Richard Smyth. The Smyth line continued until 1399. Thereafter the description in the fine was always "messuage and 23 acres of purpresture once of William Smith". It is sad to see the lands of the Smiths come to such a banal end as Roseberry House.

Whitmore Vale The name Whitmore now given to this valley which runs towards Grayshott has undergone several changes over the centuries. The same name in Tilford started as "withy more", a likely place to find such useful material. In 1370 John Thrul paid a fine of 6/8d for 2 crofts called Yslade surrendered by Robert Goudhyne. (This seems to have been part of the land that finally became Kitts [37].) The name "slade" was then commonly used for valley. The "Y" prefix suggests that the scribe had copied an earlier fine where it had been used in the past tense as Yclept. More recently, at least until Victorian times, the valley responded to the solid English "Whitmore Bottom". Today the sign off the A287 above Road Farm presents it as "Whitmoor", though at the Hampshire end it is still spelt "Whitmore".

Settlement spread up the valley as part of the general clearance of Barford. The first identifiable fine was in 1247 when Walter de fonte paid 6/8d for land. The subsequent fines show how the clearances progressed. The banks enclosing the plots along Whitmore Vale are extraordinarily well preserved. It is well worth scrambling down the steep hillside to see what was cultivated down into the late 19th or early 20th centuries. The 1870 OS map describes several as market gardens. The old road for horse and man ran along the valley side just above the banks. The present road, now opened to four-wheel traffic is modern. The idea that two vehicles could pass one another on the narrow stretch above the mills is simply ridiculous. Until the early 20th century the Barford really was a ford. The road to Headley continued up the hill on a narrow ledge cut into the hillside. This was cut away in the 1950s and the present road constructed

The spring at Whitmore Vale is located on the Headley side of the stream, close to the footpath south of a property called Springs. As there are even today, or within memory, many good springs in Churt, this one in Whitmore Vale must have been something out of the ordinary as it was used as a reference point[33]. There is of course a possibility that the spring may have formerly had a semi-religious connotation which still survived in folk memory. Close to the spring or "fonte" there was a "wolfputte". Wolfpits are not uncommon but there seems to be no general agreement whether or not the word has an animal connotation or not. There was another one in Badshot. Nearby was "Wulfrede's beam" which was used as a boundary mark in the charter of AD 909. It would be rash to do more than note the coincidence.

Notes

[1] The earliest fine relating to Welmore: 1339 5/- paid by John le Maryner for Matilda atte Ridgweye and 4 acres of purpresture. *HRO B1/92 1339*

[2] The top of Downing Street in Farnham is probably a similar example. It explains too the odd Green Lane crossing of the A287 and the Greencross Lane – Hale House Lane corner

[3] Lamentably since writing the above the old name of Hollands has been changed to Little Pitch and the signpost is now neglected and unreadable.

[4] The meaning is fowlers' brook. It was occasionally rendered as Vogelsbroc, and John le Vogel derived his name from his occupation of a wildfowler.

[5] P D Brooks, *The Frensham Tithe War*, FMSN March 1982

[6] see Appendix

[7] The Wheeler Papers consist of notes on the documents relating to the Luffes of Hide, which Miss Wheeler, a descendant of that family, deposited at the HRO.

[8] The Smiths of Barford also survived the Black Death but died out in 1399.

[9] ,A name which is hardly surprising as there had always been two of the bishop's warreners in Churt

[10] The change in spelling was first noticed when reading the Ockley transactions in the Consistory Court Rolls.

[11] Incidentally, Mayhew was a bitter opponent of the siting of the church in Churt, as being too far away from the people. His protest is in the archives of Farnham Museum.

[12] The Upfolds had been tilemakers at Farnham in the late 15th century. The will of Henry Upfold is at the HRO.

[13] Like the newman who paid recognition money in the 13th century

[14] see Appendix for description of the shearman's trade

[15] James II gave a quillette of land to the Duke of Buckingham.

[16] One meaning of hale is a tent that was erected as temporary shelter on a journey.

[17] Details from photocopied documents in the keeping of The Queen's College Oxford, kindly loaned to the writer by Sir John Hunt formerly of Hale House.

[18] see P D Brooks, *Boundary Stone at Churt*, FMSN 1981

[19] From information supplied by Mrs Devine.

[20] see also Barford page 50

[21] This is probably correct though the cottage next to Moorside was not finally demolished until after 1870.

[22] Louise Karn held her property as a tenant of the manor. Enfranchisement was the legal process of converting a tenanted property to a freehold one. A fee was charged for each enfranchisement. *Bishopric Estate books HRO*

[23] Note that he only had rights to the first cut.

[24] see Appendix

[25] A copy of the 1726 will and inventory of Thomas Newman was kindly given to me by Marion Herridge. The description of his land could fit either the first or second house but it is most probably the second one.

[26] These timbers are remarkably similar to those better preserved ones in Coppice Cottage.

[27]The Larkbys were an old family, probably more of Headley than of Churt. An earlier John Larkby's will and inventory taken on 26 October 1626 is at HRO *ref: Consistory Court 198A*

[28]One line in the 1223 Farnham Account, Sales from the Manor, even shows how the scribe collapsed at his work. *HRO B1/10 159278*

[29]FMSN Volumes Nos. 2, 3, 4, 5, 6 & 7

[30]One afternoon when chatting with former occupants about flint implements being common in Churt, the writer pointed out a nice example on a flowerbed by the lawn!

[31]Parliamentary Survey of Headley 1552 deposited at HRO

[32]The Bourne Mill at Farnham also continued to mill corn.

[33]Fines locate assarts as at the "fonte" in Churt.

Manorial Fines

The following examples of fines mostly relate to lands in Churt and are from the Farnham Accounts in the (early) Pipe Rolls and (later) Fine Books and Consistory Court Records of the bishopric of Winchester. These records are all deposited at the HRO. A full transcription of land fines for the whole manor of Farnham prior to 1348 is contained in The Bishops Tenants which is deposited at the Farnham Museum.

There may appear to be some inconsistencies in the grouping of these Churt fines which have mostly been extracted from the many hundreds in the Bishops Tenants. The obvious evidence comes firstly from the name of a land or person, though this latter may change abruptly if for instance land is acquired by marriage. The description of the small pieces of land can be particularly valuable when it regularly appears attached to a virgate or half virgate. The actual fine too may help where it continues to be the same sum or some fraction of it. Of greatest value perhaps in trying to trace the former inhabitants of Churt is an immediate knowledge of the lands described and also the latent memory of how they appeared in the original text before translation.

Notes
1. Italics have been used for additional comment.
2. O, CB. These letters represent phrases entered in front of fines.
   O: indicating whether the land owed work service to the lord.
   CB: carriage of wood to the castle for king or bishop.
3. "No heir" indicates that a new tenant has taken on the land because no heir appeared at court to pay fine. Sometimes there <u>was</u> an heir but one who could not or did not claim the land through poverty or some other reason.
4. "Increase of rent" This does not mean that the annual rent was raised but refers to a new rent from new land. It was an entry which noted that in future an increase in money would be received by the bishopric.

Crudescat (Elstead)

1235	6/8d	John of Crudescat for land and licence to marry
1244		Hugh of Crudescat for land
1246		William of Crudescat for land
1247		William of Crudescat for 2½ acres of purpresture, increase of rent
1256		William son of William for his father's land
1346		Robert Somer for a curtilage, 4 perches in length and at the far end 1 perch surrendered by Richard Crudeschate in Elstead
1340	18d	Richard Crudesat for a curtilage in Elstead, 5 perches and 1 perch surrendered by Alice Paye

Note:
There are quite a number of these small and sometimes odd shaped plots recorded in the Rolls. Some were likely to have been adjacent to a standing house, but not always. One was by a river, one at the top of Downing Street and one was for a tiny area of mowing grass (hay) in Headley.

Dye House (Elstead)

Grene – Maryner – Stynt – Paine

1308	10/-	William son of Robert atte Grene for ½ virgate at Pattifold
1338	6/8d	John atte Grene for a messuage and ½ virgate in Churt from William his brother
1340	28/-	John son of Robert le Grene for messuage and virgate from father
1349		John Grener for messuage and 1½ virgates rent due 12/6d nil paid
1350		John Grener for 2 messuages and 1½ virgates rent due 12/6d nil paid
1350	3/4d	John Maryner for 2 messuages, 1½ virgates formerly of John atte Grene (no heir)
1375		Agnes widow of John Maryner for messuage and virgate from her husband
		Robert .... for Agnes
1506	6/8d	John Marner son of Joan Marner for messuage and a virgate, toft and ½ virgate and 8 acres purpresture in Elstead late Robert Crudshott late John Marner which Elizabeth his wife held for her life which was surrendered to Thomas Luff during that time
1507	6/8d	William Stynt for messuage and a virgate, toft and ½ virgate and 8 acres purpresture in Elstead late Robert Crudshott afterwards William Marner surrendered by John son of John Marner
1546	6/8d	John Stynt for messuage and virgate, toft and ½ virgate and 8 acres of purpresture in Elstead formerly of John Maryner by surrender of Elizabeth, wife of William his father

1563	3/4d	William Wodehatch and Joan lately wife of Richard Stynt for messuage and virgate, toft and ½ virgate and 8 acres of purpresture in Elstead once of John Maryner
1563	2/6d	William Wodehatch and Joan lately wife of Richard Stynt for toft and virgate of John Maryner
1585	5/-	John Stynt heir of Richard for toft and virgate once of Thomas Maryner afterwards William Stynt
		The same for a virgate and 8 acres of purpresture
1609	6/8d	Thomas Paine for messuage and a virgate, toft and ½ virgate and 8 acres purpresture in Elstead formerly of John Waryner by surrender of John Stynt
	5/-	The same for toft and ½ virgate formerly of John Maryner

Fullbrook

1236	6d	Increase of Rent from Robert of Fulesbroc for 1 acre in the moor of Elsted
	6d	
		from Robert of Fulesbrok for his land
1298	12d	Jordan son of Gilbert of Foullchelesbrook for a house and 1d of land from his father.

Creswell

1556	12d	Richard Quinby for 1 acre of waste called Cresswell in the east of the land of Waryner

(Note: this land became part of Stock Farm)

Ridgeway

1289	2/-	Adam of Patifolde for 2 acres purpresture from Cristina of Patifolde
1311	4/-*	Robert son of Adam of Patifolde for 3 acres purpresture in Churt from Seylda** of Patifolde, mother of Adam
1313	20/-	Robert of Patifolde for a messuage and ½ virgate surrendered by Robert of Holeland in Elstead
1317	10/-	Adam son of Robert of Patefolde for a messuage and ½ virgate from his father.
1349	18d	Robert Childewell for a plot in Churt formerly held by Robert of Pattifolde *(Nobody appeared in Court when the property was 'proclaimed', it therefore fell into the hands of the Lord of the manor)*

*This is a heavy fine for such land 'out of the waste'. There were sometimes extraordinary extremes of fines amongst the ordinary ones.

**The name 'Seylda' is particularly useful as every fine down to the 19th century for the Ridgeway Farm included 'once called Zelds or Childewells' – Childewelle was a later tenant. This is one of the first names which enables identification of the early farms.

1308	6/8d	Richard atte Ruggweye from ½ virgate at Pattefold in Elstead which the men of <u>Elstead</u> used to have

1310		Matilda daughter of William atte Crouch for ½ virgate surrendered by Richard atte Rygweye in <u>Churt</u> (*on condition*) that a house is built before Michaelmas next
1332	1d	Increase of Rent from Robert atte Ridgeway for a plot in the waste in Churt 5 perches x 22 feet
	12d	Fine for above
1340	12d	above Robert for 1 acre in the marsh at Elstead surrendered by William Kingeston
		(*Note: This plot was held by Ridgeway Farm in the 19th c.*)
1349	6/8d	Richard son of John atte Ruggeweye for a messuage, ½ virgate and 9 acres purpresture in Churt from his father

Holelonde

1308	10/-	Robert atte Holelonde for ½ virgate in Patifolde in Elstead
1316	6/8d	Robert atte Holelonde for a messuage and 8 acres purpresture in Churt surrendered by Robert le Curt
1321	12d	Robert atte Holelonde for 3 acres in Churt surrendered by William atte Rygweye
1328	2/-	Matilda of Holelonde for a messuage and ½ virgate which Robert atte Holelonde once held

Punchbowl

The following are the only early fines which refer to the Punchbowl with certainty.

1283	2/-	Agnes atte Cumbe for purpresture conceded by Edith her mother
1295		William son of William le Webbe for 4 acres which Cecilia atte Cumbe had (vacant, no rent paid) (*Note: In 1311 this land was described as in Frensham*)
1310	6/8d	William, son of Stephen de Hyevyle de Patefolde for a messuage and ½ virgate in Churt from his father (*Hyevyle = High Valley*)

Upper Ridgeway

Quedhep–Luff

1363	10/-	John Quedhep for messuage and virgate on surrender of John Maryner
1375	10/-	John son of John Quedhep for messuage and virgate formerly of Thomas Lucas: no heir

thereafter see Hide Rickman-Luffe from 1503

Hide

Hide – Wayte – Letice – Luffe

1244	12d	William of Hide for ½ virgate – increase of rent
1256	12d	Robert of Hide for 1 acre

1257	3/-	Richard of Hide for his wife's land
1257	2/-	Matilde daughter of Richard of Churt for her father's land. Geoffrey of Hide, heriot one ox
1268	21d 6/8d	Increase Richard, son of John of Hide for 2 acres of moor and 4 acres of heath fine for above
1270	4/-	Richard son of Seman for Helota daughter of Robert of Clere for 4 acres purpresture
1272	2/-	Richard son of John of Hide for 6 acres of heath – increase
1283	2/-	Gunilda widow of William de la Hide for her husband's land
1283	5/-	Julia daughter of above William for ½ virgate of her father's land, which her mother resigned
1286	6d	Gunhilda of Hide for marriage of her daughter Christina
1287	3/-	Henry of Hide for ½ acre and 1 rod from Gunhilda of Hide
1298	6/8d	Richard of Hide for a messuage, virgate and a furlong and 8 acres purpresture from his father
1300	2/-	John le Turnyr for 3 acres purpresture surrendered by Richard atte Hide
1306	6/8d	John of Hide for the principal house and the other houses and lands in Churt of Richard of Hide his father
1311	10/-	John son of Richard atte Hide for a messuage, ½ virgate and half furlong containing four acres and 6 acres purpresture
1320	12/-	Roger atte Hide son of Henry for a messuage, ½ virgate, ¼ virgate and 3 acres purpresture from his father
1328	8/-	Cristina atte Hide for a messuage, virgate and 3 acres purpresture from Robert Rickman her father
1328	8/-	Richard le Reve for Cristina and her land
1349	CB	Roger atte Hide, messuage and 2 perches, virgate, 6 acres 1 rod purpresture. No rent paid
1350	CB	Roger atte Hide as above, rent due 6/10. No rent paid
1351		Roger atte Hide, as above. rent due 6/6d, paid 4d
1352		*as 1351*
1355	3/-	William Rykeman, messuage, furlong, 2 acres purpresture formerly of Roger atte Hide. Escheated as no heir presented at Court
1350	O	John atte Hide, messuage, virgate, furlong, and 18 acres purpresture. 14/-½, paid 12d
1352		John atte Hide as above gave up at Hockday through poverty
1352	6/8d	William le Wayte for a messuage, virgate, furlong and 18½ acres of purpresture q John atte Hide
1376	6/8d	Osbert atte Hegge for Agnes Wayte and a messuage, virgate, furlong and 5 (?) acres purpresture
1387	3/4d	Hugh Letice, messuage, virgate, furlong, 18 acres purpresture q. Osbert atte Hegge and Agnes his wife

| 1416 | 2/- | Thomas Houchon, messuage, virgate, furlong and 18 acres purpresture from Hugh Letice |
| | | *The property thereafter disappeared from records until 1503 – see Luffe* |

Rickman – Luffe

1320	4/8d	Robert son of John Rickman for a messuage, virgate and 3 acres purpresture from his father
1328	8/-	Cristina atte Hide for a messuage, virgate and 3 acres purpresture from Robert Rickman her father
1328	8/-	Richard le Reve for Cristina and her land
1348		Robert Rickman for a messuage, virgate and 3 acres purpresture rent due 9/1 no rent paid
1350		*as 1348*
1351		*as 1348 but* rent due 8/9d paid 4d
1410	3/4d	Agnes widow of William Rykeman for messuage, virgate and 3 acres of purpresture
1411	6/8d	John son of William Rykeman for messuage, virgate and 3 acres of purpresture
1503	2/-	Thomas Luffe for 2 crofts, messuage and virgate, 1 acre of purpresture called 'Tarpener's', 17 acres purpresture formerly of John Waite called Hidland, a croft containing 3 acres of bondland, and 6 acres purpresture, a toft and virgate and 3 acres purpresture formerly of William Rickman, a toft and virgate formerly of John Quedheppe with appurtenances called Hidemed in Tilford surrendered by John atte Rede
1525	3/4d	John, son of Thomas Luff for 17½ acres purpresture called Hydlands
1535	3/4d	William Luffe for his brother John's land at Hide (*as above*)
1560	3/4d	Alice Luff widow of John for lands (*as above*) in 1535
1562	20d	Stambridge and Alice, late wife of John Luff
1562	20d	cottage of Wheeler-Townsend (purpresture as 1535)
1583		William Luffe son of William for 4 acres purpresture parcel of 17½ acres called Hydland
1610	12d	Edward Luff for 4 acres purpresture parcel of 17 acres purpresture called Hidland by surrender of William his brother
1615	20/-	John Luffe for 7 acres purpresture at Truxford with the land of Thomas Payne on the north and Elstead common on the east by surrender of Richard Boxold

Marchants

Rickman – Tribe

| 1510 | 10/- | John Rykman heir of Richard, son and heir of William Rickman his brother and heir of said Richard, for messuage and 2 virgates which Joan widow of Richard held |

1526	13/4d	John Rickman for messuage and 2 virgates from his brother Robert. Heriot to be 2 cows worth 13/4d on death of above John
	6/8d	also for 1 virgate
1593	13/4d	Agnes Tribe wife of Thomas, sister and heir of William Rickman for messuage and 2 virgates.
	6/8d	also for 1 virgate
1597	13/4d	William Tribe for messuage and 2 virgates by surrender of Agnes
1624	13/4d	William Tribe son of Agnes for 2 virgates
	6/8d	also for 1 virgate
1664		Richard Tribe heir of William for the above

Stock Farm

Carter – Luffe

1292	6/8d	Robert son of Richard le Cartere for messuage and virgate from his father and to provide for his mother during her lifetime
1352	CB	Robert Carter for messuage and virgate: rent 8/4 paid nil
1354	3/4d	… Prat for messuage and virgate of Robert Carter
1389		… Wyghteman for messuage and virgate by surrender of John Carter
1392	12d	John Luff for a messuage and virgate
1441	12d	Thomas Pyning for a toft, curtilage, and virgate called Weightmannes by surrender of John Luffe

thereafter see Hardwyn below

Stone

1315	18d	William atte Stone for 4½ acres of waste in Churt (*rent for new land*)
		fine for above 20d
1349	6/8d	Henry Atte Stone for messuage, ½ virgate and 4 acres purpresture formerly of William atte Stone his relative
1451	6/-	William Letice for 16 acres of woodland and heath called "Carters" or "Stones". Rent for Carters or Stones 15d to be paid at Easter and Michaelmas

thereafter see Hardwyn below

(*Note: In 1451 the land had reverted to scrub. "Stock" describes the stumps of trees etc. on the re-cleared land.*)

Holelonde – Rickman – Maunt

1308	10/-	Robert atte Holelonde for ½ virgate in Patifolde in Elstead
1328	2/-	Matilda of Holelonde for a messuage and ½ virgate which Robert atte Holelonde once held
1329	5/-	William atte Hatch for Matilda atte Holeland and messuage and ½ virgate
1350		William Holonde, messuage, ½ virgate rent due 4/2 paid nil
		William atte Holeland, messuage, ½ virgate rent due 4/2 paid nil
		William atte Holeland, messuage, ½ virgate rent due 3/8 paid 6

1357	12d	Henry Blake for messuage and ½ virgate by surrender of Walter atte Holelonde no heir
1357	12d	Robert Rickeman for messuage and ½ virgate by surrender of Henry Blake
1447		Default: toft and ½ virgate formerly of John Croucher called Hollands: rent due 4/2 let to Richard Randolfe for 3/- *thereafter see Hardwyn below*

Hardwyn – Marner – Maunt

1476	3/4d	Thomas Hardwyn for messuage and virgate formerly of John Carter lately Thomas Penynge who refused the land
1476	20d	Thomas Hardwyn for toft and virgate formerly of Henry atte Stone
1476	20d	Thomas Hardwyn for virgate called Luffys
1479	20d	Thomas Marner for messuage and virgate formerly of John Carter lately Thomas Penynge who refused the land
1479	20d	Thomas Marner for toft and virgate formerly of Henry atte Stone
1479	3/4d	Thomas Marner for toft and virgate formerly of Robert Rickman called Luffs
1519	5/-	Elizabeth Mante widow of Thomas for messuage and virgate once John Carter lately of Thomas Pennyng
1519	5/-	Elizabeth Mante widow of Thomas for a toft and ½ virgate once Henry Stone lately of Thomas Hardwyn
1519	3/4d	Elizabeth Mante widow of Thomas for a toft and virgate called Luffs formerly of Robert Rickman, lately of Thomas Hardwyn and afterwards Thomas Marner

Boxall – Woods

Memorandum Farnham Manor 1719 Thomas Boxall surrenders to [blank] Woods:–

- messuage and virgate of bondland called le Hulle consisting of: Barn Field, 4 acres, Heathfield, 6 acres, House with 1 acre, Hill Field, 5 acres.
- toft and ½ virgate of bondland once of Henry Aston consisting of: one close called Woolfield, 15 acres, one close called Stockfield, 12 acres.
- toft and virgate of bondland one of Robert Rickman called Luffs consisting of: close called Broad Field, 12 acres, close called Pipers, 9 acres, close called Yew Tree, 7 acres, close called Broomfield, 5 acres.
- Also in 1720 (*all purpresture land*): Reeds, 2 acres, Creswell, 1 acre, apud Creswell Lane, 5 acres. (*Tilford Road*)

(Fig 21 shows the above fields at the time of the tithe redemption in the 19th century)

Greenhouse – Green Farm

Grene – Boxall

| 1359 | 16/8d | Julia wife of William atte Grene for messuage, 2 virgates and 6 acres of purpresture |

1515	10/6d	John Boxald for messuage and 2 virgates by surrender Robert Richman
1587	10/6d	John Boxold son of Thomas for messuage and 2 virgates called Greenhouse
1607	10/6d	Thomas Boxold son of John for messuage and 2 virgates called Greenhouse
1611	4/-	Thomas Boxold for 4 acres with cottage lately erected called Widhanger (*part of the above and surrendered by his brother John*)
1611		Thomas Boxold & Joan his wife for 8 closes beng part of 2 virgates viz: East field, 2 closes called Pyles, 1 close called le furlong, 2 closes called Haymeades, 1 close called 'the acre', 1 close called le grove by surrender of his brother John

Warryners

Waryner – Ockley

1539		John Waryner, heir of John Waryner for messuage, virgate, furlong and 4 acres purpresture, once of Hugh Letice
1560	5/6d	John Waryner for messuage, virgate, furlong and 4 acres purpresture, once of Hugh Letice, by death of his father, with licence to lease it for 21 years
1589	16d	Richard Waryner for 2 closes called Hide Reeds, 8 acres, a parcel of Edward Mant's land
1635	16d	Henry Ockley the younger for 2 closes called High Reeds 8 acres of purpresture
1635	5/6d	Henry Ockley the younger for 4 acres of purpresture called Waryners lately Thomas Waryner by surrender of father (*see also Greencroft*)

Greencroft

Wode – Wheeler/Tounsend – Luffe – Upfold

1308	5/-	John atte Wode for messuage and 6 acres purpresture from Isobel atte Wode, his mother
1348	3/-	William atte Tounsend for messuage and 6 acres from Alice atte Wode
1373	6/8d	William atte Tounsend for messuage and 3 acres purpresture formerly of William his father
1381	18d	Richard atte Ridgeway for cottage and 2 crofts containing 7½ acres surrendered by William Tounsend
1411	12d	Thomas Fre for virgate and 6 acres purpresture formerly of Thomas Oulden no heir
1433		Simon Collyne for cottage and 6 acres purpresture formerly of Peter Mylwarde no heir
1447		Default: cottage and 8 acres purpresture formerly of William Wheeler rent 2/4½d let to Simon Collyn for 16½d

1479	12½d	Thomas Letice for cottage and 6 acres purpresture formerly of William Wheeler or Tounsend called Oulden by surrender of Simon Collyne, pledge of Richard Letice for fine and repairs
1499	4d	Robert Russell for cottage and 8 acres purpresture formerly Wheeler or Tounsend which had been in the hands of the Lord for many years
1508	14d	John Padyk for cottage and 8 acres purpresture formerly Wheeler or Tounsend, lately Robert Russell by surrender of Urban Browne his son
1535	14d	Alice Luff wife of Thomas, daughter and heir of John Padyk for cottage and 9 acres purpresture formerly of William Wheeler alias Tounsend lately of John Padyk
1560	20d	Alice Luffe widow of John for cottage and 8 acres of purpresture once Wheeler or Tounsend
1562	20d	Stambridge to hold the lands of his wife Alice, late wife of John Luff for cottage and 8 acres purpresture formerly Wheeler or Tounsend
1589	14d	Thomas Upfold for for cottage and 8 acres purpresture formerly Wheeler or Tounsend by surrender of Thomas Luff
1598	14d	Walter Upfold heir of Thomas for cottage and 8 acres purpresture formerly Wheeler or Tounsend
1598	7d	Mary Upfold widow of Thomas for above

Fines for the 3 and 6 acres of purpresture on the south side of the Green Lane were difficult to separate from those of Greencross (Tounsend) and Butts (Brownes). Greencroft was at times occupied separately but more often went with the above lands. The fines suggest that Greencroft was often used as a dower house for dependants of the Tounsends, Luffes and Upfolds.

Greencross

Crouche – Tounsend

	13/4d	John de Cruce for messuage and virgate from his father William in la Cloures
1308	13/4d	Joan widow of John de Cruce for messuage and virgate from husband during widowhood
1312	13/4d	Alice daughter of John Cruche for messuage and virgate from her father
1341	13/4d	Joan daughter of John atte Crouche for messuage and virgate from her father
1341		Richard Chisman for Joan and her land
1344	12d	Joan atte Crouch for 1 acre of more from Robert atte Holeland
1344	12d	Richard atte Crouche for Joan and her land
1349		Richard atte Croucher for messuage and virgate: default of rent, due 8/4, nothing paid
1350		Richard atte Croucher rent due 4/2, 4/2 paid at Easter then gave up tenancy

1350	2/-	John atte Park for messuage and virgate in Churt formerly of above Richard, no heir
1359	10/-	William Shephurde for messuage and virgate by surrender of John atte Park
1363	4/-	William Tounsend the younger for messuage and virgate formerly of William Shephurde no heir
1470	3/4d	Thomas Penyng for messuage, curtilage, virgate and 3 acres purpresture called Townsend formerly held by Matilda daughter of Richard Penyng
1536	3/4d	Joan Brystowe widow of John, daughter and heir of Thomas Padyk for messuage, virgate, 3 acres purpresture called Townsend from Thomas
1587		John Bristowe eldest son of Richard Bristowe for Tounsend. John Holloway to have custody of John until of age

This property Townsend – now called Greencross (on east of Greencross Lane) was called "Wheeler or Townsend" about 1600 in documents and thereafter "Greencross" alone. For Wheeler see Greencroft.

Greencross – Hidland

Wayte – Lettice

1352	6/8d	Will le Wayte, messuage, virgate, furlong, <u>18½ acres purpresture</u> q. John atte Hide
1376	6/8d	Osbert atte Hegge for Agnes Wayte, messuage, virgate, furlong and 5 acres purpresture
1387	3/4d	Hugh Letice, messuage, virgate, furlong, <u>18 (acres) purpresture</u> q. Osbert atte Hege and Agnes
1447		Default of Rent. 2 tofts, a messuage, virgate; toft and 1 acre called Tarpeners, and <u>18½ acres of purpresture</u> formerly of William Wayte called Hidland which should yield 15/1½d. – nil paid *thereafter see Hide Rickman-Luffe 1503*

Butts Farm (Browns)

Fre

1411	2/-	Richard, son of Roger Fre, messuage, ½ virgate, 1 acre purpresture

Halle – Kemper – Eyre

1371	3/4d	Adam atte Halle (sic) for 10 acres purpresture and heath from John atte Hulle his cousin
	12d	John Eyre for 2 acres heath from John atte Hulle
1410	3/4d	Philip Kemper for messuage ½ virgate and 10 acres purpresture by surrender of John Eyre
1412	20d	John Eyre for messuage and ½ virgate and 8 acres purpresture by surrender of Philip Kemper

Bat – Derby – Brown – Luff – Upfold

1423	12d	Robert Bat, 2 messuages, 2½ virgates, 12 acres purpresture formerly of Robert Fre N.S.

1458	5/-	Robert Derby for messuage and ½ virgate formerly of Roger Fre lately held by John Slayford and for toft and ½ virgate and 12 acres purpresture of Hokes formerly of Joan widow of Eyre lately held by John Slayford. (*Note: John Slayford lost this land i.e. was ejected by the manorial court, because of waste and destruction and also because he let it without licence.*)
1460	3/4d	Margaret widow of Robert Derby for messuage and ½ virgate formerly of Roger Free
1535	5/6d	Alice Luff wife of Thomas, daughter and heir of John Padyk for messuage and ½ virgate q. Roger Fre and lately John Tylford: toft, ½ virgate and 12 acres purpresture at Hooks q. John Slayford and afterwards Robert Derby and lately of John Brown and lately of John Padyk
1560	3/4d	Alice Luff widow of John for messuage and ½ virgate formerly of Roger Fays (*Fre*) lately John Tilford toft and ½ virgate 12 acres at Hooks (*and Greencroft*)
1562	20d	Stambridge to hold the lands of his wife Alice, late wife of John Luff for above
1589	6/8d	Thomas Upfold for messuage and ½ virgate formerly of Roger Free lately John Tilford once of Robert Derby and afterwards John Brown toft and ½ virgate 12 acres at Hooks by surrender of Thomas Luffe

Outmoor

Andrew – Turner – Philpe – Luffe

1226	12d	Andrew for land
1257	13/4d	Robert Andrew for his father's land
1288	12d	widow of Andrew for virgate from her husband
1331	13/4d	John son of John Andrew for messuage and virgate from father
1349	5/-	John Andrew for messuage and virgate from John Andrew, uncle
1396	2/-	John Andrew for virgate and 2 acres purpresture from Richard Langford
1479	20d	Henry Turner for messuage and virgate formerly of Henry Agas called Andrews and toft where there used to be a cottage and 1 acre purpresture (*Bydens*)
1516	5/-	Richard Phylpyppes for messuage and virgate called Andrews surrender by Richard Pyner and lately held by Henry Turner his kinsman
1565	2/6d	Elizabeth Philpe widow of Thomas for messuage and virgate called Andrews
1565	5/-	John Philpe for above saving rights of Elizabeth who was to have the profits during his widowhood
1587	3/4d	Thomasina Philps for Andrews
1587	5/-	Anna Luffe daughter of Thomas Philips for Andrews and Bedowesrede

1588	5/-	Thomasina Marlion widow of Thomas Philips for Andrews which fell into the hands of the Lord because Thomas Marlion proceeded in law against John Luffe without licence from the (*manor*) court

Furlong

1257	4/-	from John Hale, Robert of Clere, Walter Allayn and David of Hale for 13½ acres in Churt – increase of rent. 4d per acre. Furlong. New rent
1670	3d	Richard Pyning for 2 parcels of land containing 1½ acres in the common furlong with cottage and barn recently erected
	1d	Richard Pyning for parcel of land containing ½ acre in common field called furlong between land of Henry Okely on east and John Bookham on west
	1d	Richard Pyning for parcel of land containing ½ acre in common field called furlong between land of John Luffe on east and John Upfold on west

Moorside

Turner – Wayte – Lettice

1341	3d	New rent from Osbert le Turner for 3 rods, 7 perches of waste in Churt
1341	12d	Fine for above
1346	13/4d	Agnes widow of Osbert le Turner for a cottage and 1 acre purpresture
1362		William le Wayte for Agnes, widow of Osbert Tourner and her cottage, etc.
1389		Hugh Letice for cottage and curtilage, ½ acre once of Osbert Turner (no heir)
1393		Thomas Court for above and 3 rods from Agnes his mother
1393		Hugh Letice for Agnes
1393	18d	Thomas Court, cottage, curtilage, croft of 3 rods by surrender of Hugh Letice

Beydens

1357	2/-	John Andrew for cottage and curtilage and 1 acre purpresture formerly Richard Beyden no heir

thereafter as Outmoor: Turner – Philipe – Luffe

Varnolds

Cuper – Carter

1285	2/-	John le Cuper for messuage and curtilage conceded by Henry Cartar
1290	12d	Agnes widow of Cartar for land in Churt
1295	12d	Julia daughter of Andrew Carter for 6 purpresture from her father

Hatch Farm *(Road Farm now Roseberry House)*

The Smiths of Barford

1252	4½d	Richard of Bereford for 1½ acres purpresture New rent
	4½d	same for fine of seisin
1257	3/7d	Richard the smith for 10½ acres and 1 perch at Bereford
1284	6d	Richard of Bereford for a third of an acre from Edith le Webbe
1284	6/8d	Richard the smith of Berford for his father's land
1291	2/-	Margaret widow of Richard the smith for messuage and 23 acres purpresture from her husband
1299	6/8d	William the smith of Bereford for messuage and 24 acres purpresture surrendered by William son of Richard
1300	6/8d	Matilda widow of William the smith for messuage and 6/- purpresture from her husband
1332	13/4d	William of Bereford for messuage and 6/9d of land from Richard his father
1332		William son of William of Bereford for messuage and 6/9d of land from his father
1379	6/8d	William Smith for messuage and 26 acres purpresture from Joan atte smythes his mother
1427	20d	Richard Figge for curtilage and 36 acres once of William smith which fell into the Lord's hand because he had no heirs

Kitts

1313	13/4d	Adam of Bereford, smith, for messuage and 15 acres purpresture and a mill from William his father
1343		increase of rent 6d Adam smythe because his land/mill straddles the stream
1343	12d	Adam le smyth for land at his mill
1343	6d	<u>Sutton Account</u>: Adam for the mill built on the borders of Surrey and Hampshire with rights to water and fishery (*mill moved to its present site*)
1344	10/-	Joan daughter of Adam le smyth of Bereford for messuage and 3 furlongs of purpresture by surrender of Adam
1349	3/4d	Richard le smyth for Joan daughter of Adam le smyth of Bereford for messuage and 3 furlongs of purpresture
1350	3/4d	William son of William the smyth for 14 acres purpresture for his mill from his father
1513	16d	Margaret widow of John Figge for messuage and 20 acres purpresture lately of Richard Godhyne

Whitmore Vale

1247	6/8d	Walter de fonte for land
1252	15d	William Crul for 2½ acres seisin
1252	15d	annual rent

1271	3/-	William Crul for 1½ acres 1 perch of heath by the Wolfputte in Churt
1271	10½d	annual rent
1272		William Crul for lengthening his ditch, rent ½d
1274	1d	Walter le Crul for a small plot next to the spring in Churt increase of rent
1274	6d	Walter le Crul for 1d of land conceded by William le Crul
1274	12d	Walter le Crul for a small plot
1288	4/-	Hugh and William sons of Walter of the spring for land worth 3/-
1288	2/-	Hugh and Richard, sons of William Crul for 1½ acres 1 rod conceded by their father
1290	5/-	Robert Crul for messuage, 10 acres and ½ acre purpresture from William his father
1296	6/8d	Richard of the spring for messuage and 8 acres from his father
1311, 1343 & 1348		*Several fines for Crul but it is uncertain whether these lands were in Hale in the Badshot tithing or the Hale lands in Churt*
1356	18d	John Threl (*name originally Crul or Prul*) for 2 acres purpresture surrendered by Richard of Bereford
1370	6/8d	John Threl the younger for croft of 2 acres called Islade by surrender of Robert Goudhyne (*Islade – in the valley – Whitmore Vale*)
1378	6d	Alexander Baret for 3 crofts of land formerly of John Threl the younger no heir
1378	6/8d	Alexander atte Brigg for a croft of 2 acres formerly of John Threl the younger no heir
1381	12d	John threl for a croft containing 6 acres purpresture from John Threl his son no heir
1414	2/-	Thomas Pyning for 3 crofts of purpresture, 6 acres and a plot of more formerly held by Alexander atte Brigg which he forfeited for waste and destruction
		Fines follow with Barford and Kitts.

The name "Crul" is one of several in which the "r" was transferred from the end of the word to the beginning. (Forst(er) became Frost). It probably derived from a nickname "Curly"; starting with Crul and Prul it finally developed into Threl

Abbreviations & Glossary

DBRG   Domestic Buildings Research Group
FMSN   Farnham Museum Society Newsletter
GMR   Guildford Muniment Room (now Surrey History Centre, Woking)
HRO   Hampshire Record Office
OED   Oxford English Dictionary
OS   Ordnance Survey
PRO   Public Record Office

acre, customary: usually smaller than the standard (statute) acre but varying in size from manor to manor; in Farnham probably about half a statute acre. For the problem of acres on the Winchester estate and conversion tables from customary to standard acres, see J Z Titow, *Winchester Yields*, Cambridge, 1972, p145–64.

amercement: penalty or fine levied at the manorial court for the various transgressions committed by the tenants, (eg trespass, fighting, theft, breaking assize). Convicted offenders were 'in the bishop's mercy' and were liable to a monetary penalty.

assart: piece of forest or grazing land converted into arable by grubbing up the trees and brushwood.

beam: Old English word for a tree

bondland: land held by a manorial tenant under the obligation to perform services for the lord.

bondwork: work which a manorial tenant was obliged to do for his lord in return for his house and land.

boonwork: work additional to customary labour service, demanded whenever necessary to complete the ploughing of the demesne, or the reaping of the corn.

close: piece of enclosed land.

defaults of rent: uncollected rent from land which was vacant or had been taken back into demesne; these were recorded year after year in the pipe rolls, often for centuries on end, and so do not necessarily refer to the year of any of the rolls in which they appear.

demesne: land held and directly managed by the lord, upon which tenants gave unpaid service according to the customs (established practices) of the manor.

enclosure allotment: piece of land allotted upon the enclosure of the common grazing land.

escheat: land which reverted to the lord on the death of a tenant without an heir, or as the result of a misdemeanour.

fine: paid on a piece of land to the bishop by the incoming tenant upon the death or withdrawal of the outgoing tenant.

furlong: the length of a furrow in a common field. Derived from *furh* furrow + *lang* long.

grange: an outlying barn.

harrowing: breaking down furrows and clods of soil on ploughed land and to cover seed etc.

hayward: the man responsible for the adequacy of stock-proof fences.

headland: the border of a field where the plough turns

heriot: a tribute paid to the lord on the death of a tenant, usually consisting of a live animal or a chattel.

hide: in Farnham, 120 acres. Originally the amount of land which could be ploughed in a year, using one plough, and which would support a family. The exact area varied according to the quality of the soil, but was generally 60 to 180 acres.

Hockday: one of the days of the year on which rent was paid – the second Tuesday after Easter Sunday.

hundred: a subdivision of a county or shire, having its own court.

mancorn: mixed corn.

manor: a feudal lordship over lands; a unit of land consisting of a lord's demesne and lands rented to tenants.

messuage: portion of land occupied by a dwelling-house and its appurtenances.

murrain: a general term for infectious disease affecting livestock.

open hall house: a timber-framed house consisting of a large room open to the roof and with a fire on the floor.

pannage: payment made to the lord for the feeding of swine in a wood.

paring: cutting a off a strip or piece.

pipe roll: medieval accounts for the bishopric estates, written on skins which were then rolled up and stored in a tube or 'pipe'.

plough boon: see boonwork.

purpresture: land of secondary quality which was not subject to the obligations placed on bondland and which could therefore be sold or exchanged more freely than bondland.

relief: payment made to the lord by the heir of a tenant holding free land upon taking up possession of the land.

rew: hedgerow

ridge and furrow: a type of field system involving parallel ridges or strips within an open field.

scabiosa: an infectious disease of livestock, possibly sheep scab.

seisin: possession of property rather than ownership; probably pre-Conquest in origin.

spud: a small narrow digging tool; to dig with a spud

statute acre: the standard acre measuring 4,840 sq yds.

tithing: the basic unit of manorial administration which by the 13th century was both a geographical as well as a social entity, to which each inhabitant over the age of twelve belonged.

toft: the land once occupied by a dwelling-house and its appurtenances.

virgate: measure of land, usually about 30 acres. The Farnham virgate was stated to be 32 acres (see *Medieval Farnham*, E Robo, 1935, p 11).

waste: inferior land used communally.

yardland: usually 30 acres.

Appendix

Lay Subsidy of 1332 for Churt

De Ada de Patteffeld	vs vjd ob	De Willelmo ate Tonesends	xvjd
De Nicholao de Patteffeld	xvjd	De Alicia ate Hale	ijs vd ob q
De Roberto de Patteffeld	ijs vd ob q	De Johanne ate Hale	xijd
De Roberto ate Ryggeweye	iijs jd ob q	De Willelmo de Putfold	viijd
De Johanne ate Ryggeweye	iijs	De Johan de Putfold	xxd ob q
De Johanne ate Hyde	ijs xd	De Johanne Kyng	xd
De Ricardo Rykeman	xxjd ob	De Ada Pype	xviijd q
De Rogero ate Hyde	xvjd	De Johanne ate Sturte	xd ob q
De Oliua Harding'	xijd	De Willelmo Fynlegh'	viijd
De Roberto le Grouere	iijs vjd	De Stephano Duryual	xijd
De Willelmo Alayn	ijs viijd	De Ricardo le Taillour	viijd
De Roberto le Cartere	xvjd	De Willelmo Coleman	xvjd
De Johanne ate Cruche	xxijd	De Johanne le Taillur	xvjd
De Sibilla ate steuenes	xxiijd ob	De Thoma Godhyue	vookd
De Henrico Thorbern	xxd	De Roberto ate Hulle	xviijd ob
De Ricardo le Foghel	iiijs xjd q	De Johanne Hunte	xxd
De Willelmo le Fre	xxd	De Sibilla le Churl	viijd
De Ricardo Alayn	xijd	De Thoma Foghel	viiid
De Johanne Marner	viijd		

Petition for grant of a copyhold

To the worshipfull Arthur Balde Esquire, Steward of the Mannor of Farnham, in Surrie, And to Richard Dennet Gent Clarke of the lands there.

Theis are to certifie, That the bearer, Richard Neale of Churt in the parish of Frinsham in the said Countie of Surrie, husbandman, is an honest ancient poore laborius man, and about Twentie yeares since, purchased a Cottage, within the said Tithinge, of one John Newman, before the said tyme longe buylt, And since by the Consent of the Tenants there, inclosed one parcell of land thereunto adjoynyng, contaynynge neere about one acre, out of the Comon Heath, neere unto a certaine bridge then called Whiteshott bridge beinge incompassed round about with the said Comon, which we whose names are hereunder wrytten, conceive it is not as yet, Neyther will be, in tyme to come, any preiudice, unto any of the Tenants, of the said Tithinge, or other of the inhabitants of the said Parish.

May it therefore please your worshipps the premisses Considered, to grant him a Coppie for the holdinge thereof, according to the Custome of the

Manor of Farnham, aforesaid, for a reasonable fyne, and, yearly rent, as you, or eyther of you shall thinke fitt, And in soe doeinge we shall rest ourselves, thankfull unto you, And be daylie bound to praye for your worshipps, healthes and prosperities.

John Luffe

The marke
Henrie . *H* . Ockley

Richard *R* Mathew

Note: This document probably dates from the last decade of the 17th century. John Luffe was probably at Greencross Farm. Henry Ockley (one of thee of that name in the 17th century) was at Warryners.

The Trade of the Shearman or Cropper

from E P Thompson MAKING OF ENGLISH WORKING CLASS page 570 Pelican 1963. The cropper's work was described before the Committee on the Woollen Trade in 1806:

"The business of a cloth worker is to take a piece of cloth in the rough state as it comes from the market, or as it comes from the market, or as it comes from the fulling mill; he first raises that cloth; after that, if it is a good piece, it is cropped wet; it is then taken and mossed and rowed; mossing is filling up the bottom of the wool after it has been cut with the shears wet, it is done with a handle set with teazles in each hand; after that it is rowed and tentered . . . and dried; if a fine piece it will receive three cuts dry after the tenter …"

After this the back was cut, and the cloth was examined for faults and repaired, brushed up, cleaned, pressed, and perhaps cut a final time. The cloth-worker or cropper undertook all these processes. Apart from the cleaning, the tentering (or stretching), and the pressing, the cropper's skill resided in the central process, by which the surface or 'nap' of the cloth was raised by means of teazles; the shearing done with very heavy hand shears (four feet in length, from handle to blade, and 40 pounds in weight). Both operations, required experience and skill. Moreover, while the croppers' wages were regulated by custom at about 5% of the value of the finished cloth, 'they can make a piece 20 pr. Cent better or worse by due care and labour or the reverse. They were thus in an unusually strong bargaining position.

Houses in Churt recorded by DBRG

Butts Farm

Greencroft

Greencross

Hale House

Hide

Marchants Farm

Moorside

Old Barn Cottage

Outmoor

Pitch Place

Redhearne

Ridgeway Farm

Squirrels

Stock Farm

Stream Cottage

The Toft

Upper Ridgeway

Woodhanger

The DBRG has added greatly to the history of post-medieval Churt by recording virtually every old house in the area. These reports are copyright of the Group but each house owner is provided with a copy of the report on their own house, both for their enjoyment as well as an aide to the preservation of their part of the national heritage. Although these reports are supplied free, most house owners usually like to make a donation since the Group is financially self supporting. The few comments on houses in the text are made from the writer's personal knowledge; and on a lighter note, the writer has been described as having seen the inside of more Churt bedrooms than anyone else in the village!

Other Books relating to the history of Churt

Churt Remembered – ISBN 0-9542486-0-0
Further Reflections on Churt – ISBN 0-9542486-1-9
Churt: an Oasis through Time – ISBN 0-9542486-2-7
– all compiled and published by Olivia Cotton

A Time of Change: a short history of Churt:
the period between 1840 and 1880
– written and published by Gillian Devine

Other Books of Local Interest

Published by John Owen Smith

Headley's Past in Pictures – ISBN 1-873855-27-3
a tour of neighbouring Headley parish in old photographs

Grayshott: the story of a Hampshire village – ISBN 1-873855-38-9
the history of Grayshott from its earliest beginnings

Walks around Headley ... and over the borders – ISBN 1-873855-49-4
a dozen circular walks from Headley, including Barford and Churt

John Owen Smith, publisher — **www.johnowensmith.co.uk**

Index

Ivy Cottage, 91
Jumps Road, 16, 67, 82, 84, 85, 87, 90
Kennel Farm, 83
Kitts, 93, 109
Lower Common, 16, 18, 57, 62
Lower Loompits, 71
Marchants Farm, 57, 59, 73, 74, 101
Maryners Lane, 70, 71, 83
Mayhew's Farm, 76
Meadows, The, 19, 82
Medieval Farnham, Robo, 11
mill, corn, 77, 92
mill, fulling, 71, 73, 77, 92, 114
mill, paper, 92
mills, at Barford, 92, 109
Minfordd, 27, 83
Moorside, 85, 108
Nether Lane, 82
Old Barn Lane, 19, 29, 76, 84
Old Forge, 34, 89, 92
Old Kiln, 9, 20, 22, 27, 71, 82, 86, 87, 88
Old Kiln Lane, 88
Old Post Office, 20, 90
Old Potters, 71
Outmoor, 14, 18, 23, 61, 77, 83, 89, 107
Outmoor Green, 85
Parkhurst, 82
Patifold, 60, 72, 98
Pipe Rolls, 9, 13, 17, 22, 31, 38, 43, 45, 53, 57, 60, 62, 96, 112
Pipers, 89
Pitch Cottage, 70
Pitch Place, 71
Pitfold, 53, 71, 77, 91
Plaster Hill, 51
plough headlands, 57, 60, 61, 62, 112
Podmore (Pudmore), 23, 76, 82, 88, 89
Pride of the Valley, 67
Queen's College, Oxford, 82

Quinnettes, 81
Redhearne, 20, 89
Ridgeway Farm, 59, 60, 72, 73, 98
ridgeways, 72
Road Farm, 93, 109
Roseberry House, 93, 109
Shant Lane, 82
Shant, The, 81
Shottermill, 13, 53
Silverbeck, 90
Simmonstone (Symondstone), 21, 91, 92
Squirrels, 23, 83
Standford, Headley, 73
Star Hill, 91
Star Inn, 91
Stock Farm, 33, 74, 75, 76, 102
Stream Cottage, 70
Tapeners, 77
Three Oaks, 85, 86
Thursley Road, 16, 70
Tilford Road, 55, 74, 84, 103
Toft, The, 29, 34, 77, 79
Truxford, 71, 76, 101
Upper Common, 16, 18, 57, 62
Upper Ridgeway, 73, 99
Varnolds, 84, 108
Warreners, 76, 104
Warreners Mead, 85, 87
Well More, 70
West Churt, 16, 55, 62, 64, 80, 89
Wey Cottage, 60, 71
Wheeler Papers, 34, 73, 77, 92
White Croft, 86
Whitmore (Whitmoor) Vale, 20, 87, 91, 92, 93, 109
Widhanger, 76, 84, 104
Wishanger, 79, 84, 91
Wolmer Cottage, 70
Woodhanger, 76, 84
Woodyers, 34, 89, 92
Wulfrede's beam, 93